LONDON 1851

1. *View from the north bank of the Serpentine in 1851. Lithograph by Brannan.*

LONDON 1851

The Year of the Great Exhibition

by

Eric de Maré

The Folio Society

London 1972

'This will long be remembered as a singularly happy year
of peace, plenty, good feeling, innocent pleasure, national
glory of the best and purest sort'.

LORD MACAULAY *Life*

PRINTED IN BELGIUM

Printed and bound by Henri Proost & Cie, Turnhout
Set in 'Monophoto' Century Schoolbook 10 points leaded 2 points
Printed throughout by lithography

CONTENTS

INTRODUCTION

LONDON has existed for nineteen hundred years. In that time its people have built certain structures so important in their lives that, even if they have survived only in records, they will never be forgotten. They have achieved iconic significance.

The first was the progenitive Bridge. The second was the defensive Wall. The third was the great Basilica, London's first town hall, built on the eastern breast of the city that had become the fifth largest trading centre in the Roman Empire. In the dark years, a church dedicated to St Paul was erected on the city's western breast that, in its fifth form, still survives there as a symbol. During the Dark Ages, too, another Christian fabric arose about a mile to the south-west of the Roman core in a damp area called Thorney Island, 'the terrible place' as a charter of 785 described it; Edward the Confessor rebuilt it together with a neighbouring palace and there the Conqueror was crowned, so setting the precedent that still links Westminster with monarchy and rule.

The Conqueror's White Tower was then built – a symbol of power as much to threaten as to defend the citizens. Centuries passed before the next icon appeared: Henry VIII's great rambling Palace of Whitehall, at the centre of which later arose London's first truly Renaissance building, the Banqueting Hall by Inigo Jones, intended to form the ritualistic centre of a new royal palace, one that was never built.

2.   *The Bridge and the Tower in the fifteenth century. From a Flemish illumination in the British Museum.*

Types of buildings and their planned arrangements, as well as single structures, have also achieved iconic status: the row of mansions with their riverside gardens that lay since mediaeval times along the Strand and where lords and prelates lived with their retinues when they came to town to attend Court or Parliament; the Inns of Court where the lawers dwelt around their greenswards conveniently situated between the centres of government and commerce; the west-end squares and domestic areas built as speculations by aristocratic landlords which belie the common misapprehension that London is a completely unplanned city; Wren's post-Fire churches with their elegant spires dominated by his matriarchal dome; the enclosed docks surrounded by their noble warehouses of the early nineteenth century lying to the east of the Tower; Nash's *Via Triumphalis*, both monumental and picturesque, that extends from the Mall right up to Regent's Park; the gentlemen's clubs around the Pall Mall area; the great termini with their attached Grand Babylon hotels of the railway age; the huge market halls of the exploding Victorian metropolis; and, last but not least, Bazalgette's magnificent granite embankments and his vast main drainage scheme that finally conquered King Cholera.

Victorian London also produced a remarkable number of single buildings that have achieved the standing of emblems: Smirke's British Museum, largest classical building in the country; Street's Law Courts in the Strand, with its splendid great hall – last of the important Gothic Revival buildings; Fowke's impressive rotunda of the Albert Hall; Scott's giant piece of facing jewellery, the Albert Memorial. These are still with us but the most important icon the Victorians built lived for only six months. This was the Great Room described by Morton Shand in the *Architectural Review* in 1937 as 'a precept as inspiring as the Parthenon, an exemplar as vital as the Pont du Gard, as important as Stonehenge or Ely Cathedral' – the Crystal Palace.

The Great Exhibition of the Works of Industry of All Nations, staged in the year Thomas Hardy called 'a precipice in time', has been well chronicled. My apologies for presenting yet another work on the subject are several. First, this is a good old story which, like a fairy tale, can bear endless and varied repetition. Secondly, no other work has shown the contents of the Exhibition and the gleaming container in their total setting, in their frame of time and place. Thirdly, no other work has had the support of so many coloured illustrations culled from contemporary prints that are little known, at least in colour, and reveal fine craftsmanship and artistry. Finally, no other work has perhaps so fully displayed what now seems to us to be visually attractive both in the fabric of London as a whole in 1851 and in the climactic gem and its displays.

We are now far enough away from that year not only to be able fully to savour its period nostalgia but also to evaluate its designs with dispassion. Often accompanied by an arrogant hilarity, stress has hitherto been laid on the vulgarity and over-ornamentation of many of the 1851 exhibits; too little has been laid on its delights, not least of those remarkable contributions that now so fascinate the industrial archaeologists – to say nothing of the products of old crafts that had reached their peaks of skilled perfection, such as carriages, cutlery, clocks and watches. This book attempts to redress the balance at a time when we are bored to desperation by our own faceless, joyless, pseudo-functional designs and are thirsting after jolly decorations for their own useless, delightful, human sake. The vogue for debunking the Victorians is well past. Their age had hideous faults but it had its virtues too, and the Great Exhibition was their symbol. At least the age, unlike our own, possessed supreme self-confidence and felt, with an enviable innocence, that it knew where it was going.

What happened to this country in particular and to the world in general during the seminal year of 1851? The Corn Laws and the Navigation Laws had been repealed and land-owners had been mollified by easy loans; the Chartist Riots and the rick burnings of the 'forties were well over, Free Trade was on the wing, the young queen was popular and mob violence of the 'dangerous classes' was no longer greatly feared by those who were well-heeled. That a great international exhibition should be held at this time in London, and for the first time in the world, was a natural result of the Industrial Revolution England had fathered; the time was ripe for providing a huge shop window for the display of new skills and manufactures that could capture the expanding mass markets. The Great Exhibition was, in fact, a triumphant monument to Free Trade, for in her political and economic supremacy Britain did not yet fear foreign competition. As a French visitor to the Exhibition, M. Lemoinne declared: 'With steam and the Bible, the English traverse the Globe'. The Great Exhibition was also the monument to *Pax Britannica* because Free Trade meant above everything peace between nations. 1851 was a year of general goodwill and of unquestioning faith in the future.

England was in a state of transition between the old

3. *All the world going to see the Great Exhibition. Etching by Cruikshank.*

quiet world of farming and the humming new world of industry that had perforce to be concentrated in towns together with its machine-minding serfs. Half the country's population of nearly twenty-one millions were already urban dwellers and of those over two and a quarter millions lived in London. No one was prepared for this sudden urban influx or for the drastic changes that were occurring – any more than we are prepared today for the effects of the Second Industrial Revolution of cybernetics, automation and atomic power.

In spite of the Great Reform Act of 1832, franchise was restricted to owners of property and, even in 1851, government was still largely drawn from the old land-owning aristocracy. Social legislation on matters that affected the whole community – such as water supply, main drainage and interment – was still ineffectual in spite of the heroic but unpopular efforts of men like Edwin Chadwick and Lord Shaftesbury. The national revenue was paltry, amounting in 1851 to a mere fifty million or so; Income Tax was only 3p in the pound and even the desirability of that tax was moot. Every man was expected to fend for himself in a world of competitive self-help and *laissez-faire*, in the irrational faith that God helps those who help themselves – by hard work, continent living, and the thrift that accumulates capital. In the evangelical mood of the times, religion and material progress were interwoven, for if a man was successful in business enterprise be was surely favoured by the Deity of the Protestants. Darwin had not yet exploded his cerebral bomb to disturb the complacency of the simple fundamentalists.

A wave of prosperity rendered the early fifties the most optimistic years of the century, for the general fall in prices benefited everyone and employment was easy to find. Industry was still small in scale and run by individuals and families rather than by boards and combines, not least in London which was not only the centre of government, a great world port, a trading centre and a capital, but – as is not often realized – the largest manufacturing town in the country. Although the Bank Charter Act had been passed in 1844, the credit monopolists did not yet fully dominate government and industry; the old National Debt, though large enough, was not yet astronomical in size, while rapid capital expansion allowed the nation as a whole to distribute enough buying power to its consumers to sell all it could produce. If labour was now ruthlessly divided, many traditional handicrafts still flourished – as the Great Exhibition, despite its many courts of machinery, revealed. Thanks to its coal, iron and inventive flair, combined with the exploitation of cheap labour and the single-minded ambitions and incentives that generate energy, Britain was far ahead of the rest of the world in its industrial expansion.

In 1851 women were no longer working in the coal-mines. In that year, Shaftesbury's Common Lodging Houses Bill was accepted — 'the best Act', thought Dickens, 'ever passed by an English legislature'. The new Board of Health and the co-operative movement were in being. The felicitous shade of Jeremy Bentham went marching on, and although Marx was not taken seriously, socialism already possessed its respectable Christian wing. The Welfare State existed in embryo and, as the years passed, managed by a hair's breadth to save uncontrolled *laissez-faire* from itself. In spite of the poverty and degradation of the urban masses, England in 1851 seemed peaceful, prosperous and secure,

4. *The Crystal Palace from the north-west. Litograph by Ackerman.*

and even to those who in Carlyle's famous phrase had 'the liberty to die by starvation', emigration to the expanding colonies offered hope.

In 1851 the Window Tax was repealed, the first submarine telegraph cable was laid between Dover and Calais, Scott Archer introduced his collodion wet plate to photography, the Crown enclosed and planted ten thousand acres of the New Forest, Stephenson's tubular railway bridge across the Menai Straits was in working order, W.H.Smith had established his railway bookstalls, and the first Public Libraries Act had been passed. Mrs Gaskell's *Cranford* was being serialised in Dickens's magazine, *Household*

Words, and publications of the year included Melville's *Moby Dick*, Ruskin's first volume of *Stones of Venice*, and Harriet Martineau's shocking *Letters on the Laws of Man's Social Nature and Development*. Harriet Stowe's *Uncle Tom's Cabin* and Roget's *Thesaurus* were in the press and Mary Ann Evans, *alias* George Eliot, was appointed assistant editor of the *Westminster Review*. The great Macready made his last stage appearance as Macbeth, Mrs Bloomer from the United States toured England to advocate her National Dress of pantaloons, an Act was passed declaring that ecclesiastical titles conferred by the Pope in Britain were illegal, Landseer painted his 'Monarch of the Glen', Daguerre and Turner died, Oliver Lodge was born, Oscar Wilde's parents were married, Cambridge beat Oxford at cricket and Henry Groom was publicly executed at Norwich.

In 1851 gold was discovered in Australia and a quarter of a million sheep were grazing in New Zealand; in Africa the Kaffir War was on and Livingstone reached the Zambesi. Sweden and Norway were joined under a single monarchy, and, although the Russian serfs were not yet emancipated, the St Petersburg-Moscow Railway was opened.

In London, Nash's Marble Arch was transferred from the front of Buckingham Palace to its present site on the north-east corner of Hyde Park, Holloway Prison was finished and the Record Office begun, and the Royal School of Mines was founded. But the greatest event of the year, not only in London but in the whole country, indeed in the world, was, of course, the Great Exhibition of All Nations held in Hyde Park within its enormous box.

5. *Bloomerism – an American custom. Punch 1851.*

METROPOLITAN BACKCLOTH

THE Sixth Census in 1851 found London's population to be 2,363,405. Within the next twenty years it was to grow by nearly a million and, by 1881, it had reached 4,764,312; in spite of high death-rate, it doubled within a generation. A large part of this growth was due to the continuing influx from the surrounding countryside and from abroad, an influx that helped to stay the degeneracy of the half-starved, gin-sodden stock of the rookeries that became sterile by the third generation.

Although its Victorian growth was so explosive, London had been expanding for centuries around the ancient Square Mile of the City, an expansion that had always been watched with a certain distrustful awe. In the 1720's, for example, that indefatigable reporter Daniel Defoe had described Chelsea as a Town of Palaces which 'by its new extended buildings seems to promise itself to be made one time or other a part of London, I mean London in its new extended capacity . . . If it should so happen, what a monster must London be.' A century later London had become Cobbett's 'Great Wen' and, by 1851, Dickens's 'Great Oven'. The expansion had begun in the Liberties outside the Wall and around the bridgehead in Southwark. Then the grounds of the row of palaces between the City and Westminster lying along the Strand were mostly built over, while the poor districts expanded for miles around the dockland to the east and the wealthy districts expanded in the opposite direction. So was formed in time the exist-ing pattern of City core, East End, West End and that sprawl of South London the new bridges and railways of the nineteenth century encouraged. As the Wen spread over the primeval marshes the outlying villages became absorbed into the brickwork obesity of the tolerant, undisci-plined and grubby carcass that is Greater London.

Yet even as late as 1851 London would have seemed to us to possess a visual comprehensibility and cohesion that have long since vanished. It was still comparatively calm

6. *Regent's Circus, Oxford Street. "The World's Metropolis".*

and classical in character, human in scale and unified by an established grammar of design that included the so-called Georgian sash window. Many merchants still lived with their families above their counting-houses in the City, but before long all their homes there would become offices. As any map of the time will show, the main coaching roads that radiated from the centre like the tentacles of an octopus were built up along their fringes for many miles, but in between them spread farms and market gardens among which, here and there, lay some old rural parish around its green and duck-pond. So, in 1851, an afternoon's carriage drive or a hacking into the open country were still possible from any point in the metropolis. Hampstead and Highgate were clearly articulated villages; so were Westbourne Green, Kensington, Earl's Court and Walham

Green on the west, while to the north and east Stoke Newington, Upper Clapton, Homerton, Hackney, Old Ford, Bow and Bromley were surrounded by commons and open fields; the Isle of Dogs was still largely marshland, while Leyton and Walthamstow were right out in the country. *The British Metropolis*, published in 1851, describes Acton, Barnes, Battersea, Chiswick, Clapham, Hammersmith, Dulwich and Hornsey all as villages, and it picks out Hampstead as 'a village famous for its medicinal waters'.

London in 1851 was far more shapely than it was to become in the following decades when all cohesion was disrupted by cheap speculative housing, by a confused multiformity of scale and style in the more monumental buildings, and by the railway extensions on their arched approaches that ran almost to the centre of the town. Disruption began that very year with the opening of Victoria Street running from Westminster towards Vauxhall Bridge Road, the basin of the Grosvenor Canal and the Chelsea Water Works where Victoria Station was to stand. As the buildings rose on either side, it was to become within twenty years, as Tennyson described it, 'like a street in Hell' – partly due, no doubt, to the melancholia that any street arouses whose width is the same as the height of its buildings.

In spite of squalid casbahs like that of St Giles – which Dickens fictionalised in *Bleak House* (1853) as the fever-haunted Alsatia of Tom-all-Alone's–the West End possessed a good deal of serene cohesion, for the Battle of the Styles was not yet fully joined. There lay the lordly estates with their formal squares where the plane trees were reaching maturity – 'the great and peculiar beauty of London' as a foreigner described them in the 1830's. Between them ran

7. *The Quadrant, Regent Street.*
Lithograph of 1852 from a drawing by E. Walker.

8. *Hackney in 1851. Lithograph by G.J. Pope.*

Nash's spinal cord, brilliantly kinked at All Soul's Church with its pencil-point spire where the top of Regent Street turns into Portland Place.

Regent Street was lined with fashionable shops, many of which sold the clothing that formed so important a part of middle and upper class rituals, particularly in times of mourning. It was to remain fashionable throughout Victoria's reign. Yet in 1851 an important stretch of it, that pleasant Quadrant curving up from Piccadilly Circus, had already been architecturally debased; in 1848 Nash's protective arcading with its Doric columns of cast iron was removed, partly because it darkened the interiors of the shops and partly because it served as a lurking place for street walkers, 'Cyprians of the better sort' as Mayhew called them. Much protest was aroused when its removal was proposed, but in the end the shopkeepers won the day. That fecund Victorian journalist, George Augustus Sala, in his *Twice Round the Clock* (1859) described Regent Street as 'an avenue of superfluities – a great trunk-road in Vanity Fair' and he asked:

'Whatever could have possessed our Commissioner of Woods and Forests to allow those unrivalled arcades to be demolished? The stupid tradesmen, whose purblind, shop-till avarice led them to petition for the removal of the columns, gained nothing by the change, for the Quadrant, as a lounge in wet weather, was at once destroyed; it not only afforded a convenient shelter beneath, but it was a capital promenade for the dwellers in the first-floors above. The *entresols* certainly were slightly gloomy; and moustached foreigners, together with some gaily-dressed company still naughtier, could with difficulty be restrained from prowling backwards and forwards between Glasshouse

9. *London Br*

August 1851.

Street and the County Fire Office. But perambulating Regent Street, at all hours of the day and night, as I do now frequently, I see no diminution in the number of moustached or rouged, or naughty faces, whose prototypes were familiar to me, years agone, in the brilliant Quadrant.'

On the whole Londoners came to dislike their Georgian inheritance, regarding its terrace housing in particular, such as that of Gower Street, as possessing a dull uniformity. The prospering middle classes, products of industrialism, wanted value for money in their buildings in the form of ample space and lavish application of cosmetics; they wanted to express their competitive individualism and to find escape from the industrial squalor they were introduc-

ing into the romance of a stylistic dreamland. And perhaps they were making a protest of envy, too, against the educated restraint of the Palladian tradition that had been fostered by the old, exclusive cabal of the landed aristocracy. Had they respected that tradition, the Arcades of the Quadrant might have been spared.

Sala's 'naughty faces' hint at the enormous amount of open prostitution that prevailed in Victorian London and shocked foreign visitors. Known as the Great Social Evil against which vast sums were spent in futile propaganda by a number of righteous organizations, this free trade in bodies was a by-product of the appalling poverty of the New Babylon, and it tended, like robbery without violence, to fluctuate in extent with the ups and downs of the trade cycle.

As the swan song of the domestic tradition of the eighteenth century, two wide areas were still being built in 1851 to form pleasant architectural links between Georgian and Victorian London – Belgravia with Pimlico, and the districts to the north of the Uxbridge Road between Marble Arch and Shepherd's Bush. Detailing had become coarser, but a stuccoed overall elegance, homogeneity and a coherence of scale remained together with formality of lay-out around generous green spaces. The terraced houses were large and possessed mews stabling near at hand for the carriage folk. Here large families could be reared both by the old patricians and the rising Forsytes with their capital carefully cossetted in Consuls.

Belgravia and the less fashionable area of Pimlico to its south were the products of the great speculative builder Thomas Cubitt; built on ducal land they were the largest planned development London achieved until the post-war

10. *Cheyne Walk and Cadogan Pier*
before the Chelsea Embankment was built. Engraving of 1860.

11. *Charles Fowler's Hungerford Market. Contemporary lithograph by J. Harris.*

12.   *Hungerford Bridge and North*

scheme at the Barbican. Happily it remains to a large extent still intact, even if Pimlico was ruthlessly divided from Belgravia when the railway lines crossed the river and ran into Victoria Station during the late 'fifties. Begun in the 1820's, Belgravia was not fully completed even by 1851. Nor, indeed, was another estate in which Cubitt was involved – that of the Duke of Bedford in northern Bloomsbury, for Gordon Square was not in full occupation until 1860. Another estate owned by Bedford was Fig's Mead, or Bedford New Town as it came to be called, but in this Cubitt did not participate. It was a late development and unusual in being conceived for the lower-middle and artisan classes as a model suburb; begun in 1830, it was not complete in 1851, and, although it was an excellent and benevolent scheme, the arrival of the London and Birmingham Railway in 1834 disrupted the planning.

Beyond the Gravel Pits at Notting Hill Gate, the racing track called the Hippodrome had ended its brief existence and, typical of the new age, a Gothic revival church had been erected where the grandstand had stood at the top of Ladbroke Grove, while around it the classical terraces, squares and crescents were growing with their Tuscan porticoes, ornamental ironwork and basement areas. Here much of the old racing track had been retained to form spacious communal gardens between the houses.

Such planned areas were privately conceived, for London had no central government that could make adequate planning and housing official. Only the City itself possessed any degree of organisation, and the rest of the Wen lacked any adequate control even in sanitary affairs. London in 1851 was far from healthy, and cholera, typhoid, typhus, dysentery and other diseases were endemic until the Metropolitan Board of Works began to bring improvements after 1855. In that year the metropolis was still under the confused jurisdiction of no less than three hundred uncoordinated authorities and, not until 1889, when the London County Council began its operations, did London achieve an effective government.

Let us open the admirable, coloured map produced in 1851 by James Wyld, Geographer to the Queen and a character we shall meet again. There lies the Crystal Palace vividly marked with a dash of vermilion just to the north-west of the Knightsbridge Barracks on that wide patch to the south of Rotten Row where footballs now spin on wintry afternoons. The map is spotted with areas of green to indicate the parks, squares, gardens and cemeteries; the Oval is there and so is the large area of Victoria Park to the east. The rivers and docks are in pale blue and we can now begin a river journey, setting off from the old, picturesque timber bridge of Battersea built in 1771 and immortalised in Whistler's famous nocturne in the Tate Gallery showing fireworks from Cremorne flashing in the sky between the silhouetted timbers.

The river varied greatly in width and flowed more slowly than it does today, for the containing embankments had not been built. Cheyne Walk ran along the river bank as in any Georgian township on the upper Thames, and further to the east the grounds of Chelsea Hospital ran to the riverside. On the south bank here lay the market gardens of Battersea Fields, for the public park was not yet in existence, and beyond them the Southampton Railway ran to Nine Elms Terminus. Chelsea Suspension Bridge was still only a project and the next bridge we would see would be Vauxhall running south into Kennington Lane beside the old Vauxhall pleasure gardens; completed in 1816 to the design of James Walker, this was the first iron bridge to cross the river. Beyond the bridge, on the north bank where the Tate Gallery now stands, an enormous structure arose with corner turrets topped by conical roofs like a French fortress. Although it makes a pretty star-shape on the map, this was a grim building – the dreaded Tench or National Penitentiary of Millbank, completed in 1821, and based on Jeremy Bentham's principle of the Panopticon or Inspection House, wherein a large number of people could be kept under observation from a central point. Bentham, in fact, had bought the site himself on which to erect his model prison – one, indeed, that was badly needed to replace the notorious prison hulks down-river that had become the despair of penal reformers.

The Tench was all of yellow brickwork founded on a concrete raft to bear its weight on the bogland; it took ten years to build and several architects were involved in its difficult construction. With its six radiating pentagons, its thousand cells and its three miles of corridors, it finally covered sixteen acres. Half a mile to the north-west of the Tench stood another grim gaol, that of New Bridewell or Tothill Fields, on a site now occupied by Westminster Cathedral. Under the Prison Acts of 1865 and 1877, life in such places of detention was soon to become a cruel purgatory for the well regulated promotion of misery. There isolation combined with the purely punitive penances of treadmill, cranks, shot drill and oakum picking all too often turned criminals into lunatics.

Beyond the new Houses of Parliament, still not completed and lacking their two main towers, Labeleye's graceful stone bridge of 1750, already in serious decay, crossed the

13.　*View of the proposed St. Katherine's Docks by Thomas Telford. "Gentleman's Magazine" 1826.*

river with fifteen leaps. A short reach further on a new bridge was in being – the simple work of iron suspended between two Italianate towers, erected in 1845 and called the Hungerford. Its designer was I.K. Brunel, who among other works had built the Great Western Railway and was to build the *Great Eastern* steamship. He also designed the Clifton Suspension Bridge across the Avon Gorge: completed after his death, this contained the chains from the demolished Hungerford Bridge.

That bridge ran from Lambeth straight into one of London's most monumental buildings and one of considerable character – the classical, galleried, symmetrical structure of stone of Hungerford Market by Charles Fowler, who also designed the Covent Garden Market. Here, for some time, vegetables, fish and poultry were sold. Built in the early 1830's, it survived for only thirty years and was demolished in 1862, together with the bridge, to make way for the new Charing Cross station, hotel and railway viaduct. The market had originally been erected as a speculation by the Hungerford family, owners of the burned-down Durham House (one of the old Strand palaces), but it did not flourish even after the bridge had been built. By 1851 some alterations had been made: the fish market was covered over with glass and was being used as a diorama, while the main hall was converted to a bazaar with a theatre above it.

Below Hungerford Market, the York watergate of 1626, standing today at the back of the Embankment Gardens, formed from land reclaimed when the Victoria Embankment was built, was still lapped by the tide in 1851. A few hundred yards down river stood the Adelphi terraces with their riverside promenade – the speculative housing scheme of the Adam brothers that, apart from a few relics, vanished some decades ago.

At the bend of the river stood Waterloo Bridge, one of the three crossings of London's river designed by John Rennie. Completed in 1817, its fine span of nine elliptical arches was decorated with pairs of Doric pilasters. At its north bridgehead, Somerset House, London's first great office block, stood right on the riverside, but, though begun in the eighteenth century, its western end had not yet, by 1851, been completed.

Only three more bridges followed: Robert Mylne's Blackfriars, opened in 1769 as the third to be built across the river and demolished in 1863; Rennie's Southwark, completed in 1819, as the largest bridge of iron that had yet been constructed and having only three spans with spandrels of open, diamond pattern; and finally Rennie's New London Bridge of stone, now re-erected in Arizona.

Thus, in 1851, London possessed no less than eight road bridges, all but one of them being Georgian. A ninth could be added if we include William Tierney Clark's elegant suspension of 1827 lying upstream at Hammersmith which was not replaced by the present structure until the 1880's. Its appearance can be judged by the delightful, though smaller, bridge at Marlow which was conceived by the same engineer. No railways yet crossed the river, for the first railway boom was over and the second boom of the sixties that carried the iron horses right into the town had yet to come. So rapid was London's growth to be in the following decades that, by 1870, three new road bridges were either completed or under construction and five new railway bridges had appeared.

One other river crossing existed in 1851, but this was

14. *The Thames Tunnel. "The World's Metropolis".*

below ground – Sir Marc Isambard Brunel's double tunnel between Wapping and Rotherhithe. The first of its kind to be built and a heroic achievement for its time, it had been opened in 1843 after eighteen years of calamitous effort. The younger Brunel was involved in its construction and, in one of the floodings, nearly lost his life. The intention had been to build carriage ramps down to the Great Bore as it came to be called, but this was never done and eventually the tunnel was – and still is – used for a railway. The great enterprise was a sad failure financially: in 1851 there was only footway, of little use except as a tourist attraction where, in the endless rows of alcoves, lit by jets of gas, stood stalls where women offered for sale views of the tunnel, cheap jewellery, sweets and ginger beer.

Beyond the Custom House and the Tower, the new enclosed docks began: St Katherine's, London, New Dock and then, joining the reaches of Lime house and Blackwall above the Isle of Dogs, the West India Docks. Further east still, by the River Lea, the East India Docks were in

working order, but the Victoria, first of the Royal Group on the far side of the Lea, was not yet in existence: it was not opened until 1855. On the south bank a complex that included the Commercial and the Surrey existed mainly for the timber trade, and south of them ran the abortive Grand Surrey Canal reaching no further than Camberwell Road. Squalid and impoverished as the whole dockland area was, its waters sprouted a romantic forest of masts: the beautiful tall sailing ships of wood had not yet been ousted by the squat steam ships of iron. Indeed, as late as the 1870's, more than twice the number of ships arriving at the Port of London were still under sail, although many were by then using steam as well. Up river, however, the situation was different; there the water was alive with penny paddle steamers used for local passenger transport, particularly by commuters during rush hours, in spite of the stench of the river, which had virtually become an open sewer for the whole metropolis. All local cesspits had been abolished in 1847, producing a dangerous situation that was not to be cured until nearly twenty years later when Bazalgette's main drainage was completed.

What of the land traffic in 1851? Most people walked to work: cheap workmen's fares had not yet been instituted and the knife-board horse buses could be afforded only by the middle classes, who also used the four-wheeled growlers, the speedier, two-wheeled hansom cabs and private equipages. By 1851 traffic jams were already fairly serious at certain places at commuting hours and they were not helped by the driving of livestock through the streets to the markets at any time of day, a nuisance that was not controlled until a statute of 1867 forbade this between ten in the morning and seven in the evening. The

15. *Buildings on the east side of Regent's Street.*
Contemporary print.

droppings of this livestock, combined with those of the horses (one of which deposits at least six tons in a year) explains why the crossing sweeper figures so prominently in Victorian literature.

The huge success of the Great Exhibition would not have been possible without the existence of the new railways and, in 1851, London already possessed a good deal of railway communication, at least on its outskirts. The first railway of the metropolis had been completed in 1836 and ran for four miles in a straight line on 878 brickwork arches from London Bridge to Greenwich. The Croydon Railway, linked to it, followed three years later, terminating at the Bricklayers' Arms Station in the Old Kent Road. In the forties the Birmingham line of the London and North-Western Railway, now controlling five hundred miles of permanent way, arrived at a Euston Station whose magnificent Doric entrance propylaeum and great hall by Hardwick were so brutally and needlessly murdered in 1962 to make way for the present sterile inconvenience. To its east the plainer and more functional King's Cross by Lewis Cubitt was nearing completion in 1851, and so some miles to the west was Paddington Station, the terminus of Brunel's broad-gauge Great Western Railway that ran to Bristol. Here a hotel, the first of its gigantic kind, was built, designed by Hardwick in a symmetrical Frenchified style, and this hotel still stands today.

At Chalk Farm, the London and Birmingham line sent a branch right across the north of London which, turning down south round Victoria Park, ended at the West India Docks. Crossing it at Bow, the Eastern Counties Railway terminated north of the City at Shoreditch, while at Hudson New Town to the north of Stratford it branched off to the

north-east as the Northern and Eastern Railway. Another branch ran south-west at Old Ford to join the Blackwall line that ran from the east right into the City to Fenchurch Street. The Blackwall Railway, like the Greenwich, ran on arches – a costly system tending to increase the squalor of London's poor areas, but one which was needed not only to maintain a level approach but to avoid innumerable level crossings at street level. The Blackwall Railway, completed in 1840, was an eccentric in that the carriages initially ran on an endless rope powered by stationary steam engines.

South of the river the Southampton Railway ended, as we have seen, at Nine Elms but a branch line extended further east to Waterloo Road and a large brewery that became Waterloo Station. The London Brighton and South Coast Railway was not completed till 1854, but it then became useful to the promoters with its excursion line to the Crystal Palace at Sydenham.

The railways made the gargantuan growth of London

16. *King's Cross terminus of the Great Northern Railway.*
I.L.N. Oct. 1852.

17.   *Manchester in 1851. Etching by Cruikshank.*

possible but, like the modern motorways, they did so by wrecking civilized urbanity, particularly in the later developments of the sixties when the lines began crossing the river and several new termini were built. As John Kellet notes in *The Impact of Railways on Victorian Cities*, 'In London something of the order of 800 acres of central land was taken for railway use in the course of the nineteenth century; an area sufficient for a fair sized town in itself.' The worst effects of this railway expansion was the uncontrolled packing of the poor, particularly around King's Cross, St Pancras and Euston, and only a certain amount of government interference, exercised in spite of the *laissez-faire* economy, prevented London's being torn to pieces by competitive railway enterprise. At least, in the end, that oval heart of London containing the major parks and the old squares, measuring about four miles wide and a mile and a half deep, was saved from railway penetration. On the other hand, the roads were thereby rendered more crowded in that inter-terminal traffic was, as it remains, considerable – a problem mitigated to some extent by the building of the underground railways in the sixties and the completion of the Inner Circle in 1881.

How did the Great Exhibition directly affect the metropolis in that lively summer of 1851? No less than 6,063,986 entries to the exhibition were recorded during the 140 days it was open, and, allowing for several visits by many people, about four million individuals must have travelled to Hyde Park at least once. The daily round of the town was thereby noticeably animated. Most visitors came from the provinces but many also arrived from abroad, an invasion greeted by Charles Dickens in his *Household Words* with pleasure:

18.   *London in 1851. Etching by Cruikshank.*

'I am of the opinion that the editors of the foreign newspapers will no longer declare that we live on raw beef-steaks, and occasionally eat the winners of our Derbies; that every nobleman takes his 'bouledogue' to court with him; that we are in the daily habit of selling our wives in Smithfield market; and that during the month of November three-fourths of the population of London commit suicide. Altogether I think that a little peace, and a little good-will, and a little brotherhood among nations will result from the foreign invasion.'

The bus companies – all at that time, of course, run by competitive private enterprise – made the most of the situation and their employees worked for seventeen hours a day in all weathers. The *Daily News* complained of 'the increasing exactions and insolent conduct of the omnibus people'. On wet days 'they absolutely run riot, refusing passengers for less than a shilling fare, and those which are appointed to run to long distances, such as Kennington and Islington, actually declining passengers for those distances at any price, in order that they may make short journeys to Charing Cross for which they insist on the full fare.'

The railway companies now initiated the excursion train, one of the organizers being young Thomas Cook. To some extent the companies were compelled to reduce their fares in competition with cheap sea trips along the coasts, and in time a return ticket from the West Riding of Yorkshire to London dropped to five shillings (25p). Some people walked to London along the empty country lanes, including one Mary Callinack, who, though aged eighty-five, arrived on her feet from Penzance with a basket on her head - 'a most hale old woman' wrote the Queen in her Exhibition Journal that described her many visits to the Crystal Palace, 'who was almost crying from emotion, when I looked at her'.

Crowds arrived not only from the manufacturing towns but from market towns and villages, either singly, in families, or in throngs. As Queen Victoria recorded on June 14th:

'Quite forgot to mention that on the morning of the 12th we saw 3 whole parishes, Crowhurst, Linchfield and Langford, from Kent and Surrey (800 in number) go by, walking in procession 2 and 2, the men in smock frocks, with their wives looking so nice. It seems that they subscribed to come to London, by the advice of the clergyman, to see the Exhibition, it only costing them 2s and 6d.'

Accomodation in hotels, boarding houses and spare rooms became more and more difficult to find as the months went by, and prices for bed and board rose accordingly. The Commissioners did lend a helping hand but only to the extent of opening a register of anyone disposed to provide rooms. Tallis declared:

'The commissioners were wise in leaving the accomodation of the strangers to the care of the town itself, and innumerable were the various residences that opened their doors to those that sought a temporary abode . . . Among other accomodations that were provided, through the speculation of spirited individuals, we may notice a "monster" establishment for the reception of the working-classes, projected and registered by Mr Thomas Harrison, of Ranelagh Road, Pimlico . . . The building was in the immediate vicinity of Mr Cubitt's Pimlico Pier, to which steam-boats arrive from the city every ten minutes. It occupied a space of two acres, was bounded by roads on

19. Looking for lodgings. "This is all I have Ma'm".
Etching by Cruikshank.

three sides, was airy, and well ventilated. It contained two sleeping rooms, comprising an area of 25,000 feet and two other dormitories of half the size. These four rooms were calculated to accomodate 1,000 persons per night. Every lodger had his own bedroom, separated from the others by a partition seven feet high, ensuring perfect privacy to the occupant. Efficient warders were appointed to watch over the dormitories, which were well lighted with gas during the night ... In each room was a good bed, and the lodgers kept the keys of their own dormitories. Each of these rooms was five feet wide and six and a half long. The dining-room, the reading-room, and the smoking room, had each an area of 2,000 feet. The news-room was well supplied with newspapers, magazines, and all works relating to the Exhibition, and other sights of London, free of charge. A band of music enlivened the reveries of the smokers in their cloudy appartment. On the summit of the edifice was a lantern 1,500 feet square, from which visitors were enabled to enjoy an excellent view of the moving panorama of the river and the adjacent country. Hot rolls were baked upon the premises, and a good breakfast provided for 4d, and a dinner for 8d [say 1½p and 3p]. The price of the lodging, with all the agréments and advantages, was 1s 3d per night [about 6p], which also included soap, towels and every convenience for ablution. "Boots" performed his duty for a penny each and a barber looked after the heads and chins of the guests. A surgeon was also in daily attendance at nine o'clock. A penny omnibus was attached to the service of the institution ...'

Vivid pictures of the London scene in 1851 have been drawn by one who was there, none less than Henry Mayhew. Let a few extracts from his *1851 or the Adventures of Mr and Mrs Sandboys and Family who came up to London to Enjoy Themselves and to see the Great Exhibition*, which was illustrated with etchings by George Cruikshank, conclude this chapter:

'Every city was arranging some "monster train" to shoot the whole of its inhabitants, at a halfpenny per ton, into the lodging-houses of London ... Not a village, a hamlet, a borough, a township, or a wick, but had each its shilling club, for providing their inhabitants with a three days' journey to London, a mattress under the dry arches of the Adelphi, and tickets for soup *ab libitum*.'

Eventually the Sandboys of Buttermere with their two

20. Omnibus to the Great Exhibition. Etching by Cruikshank.

servants reach the Metropolis 'without any further misadventure than being informed, on their arrival, that there
was not a bed to be had within five miles for love or money.'
At the Bull and Mouth, 'to their great astonishment they
found a large placard exhibited, inscribed with the following terrible announcement – "The Beds Here are Quite
Full" '. Mayhew continues the tale of misadventure:

'Arrived at the residence of the lady indicated by the
gentleman who superintended the supply of provisions to
the inmates of the Bull and Mouth, Mr and Mrs Sandboys
were asked to step into the passage (the lady apologizing
for the parlours being both full), and there Mrs Fokesell,
whose husband, she was happy to say, was at sea, informed
them, to their great horror, that she had only one hammock
left unoccupied; and if the lady and gentleman thought
they could make shift with that until such time as they
could meet with anything better, why it was at their service
for five shillings a night. The young lady and the female
servant Mrs Fokesell might perhaps accomodate in her
bed, and if the footman wouldn't mind lying on the knife-
board, and the young gentleman thought he could pass
the night comfortably on the top of the grand piano, why

she would do everything in her power to make them comfortable.'

And so on in the ponderous humour of the period, Pickwick style, indicating with truth that London was rather short of accomodation during the months the 'Great Glass Hive', as Mayhew called it, was open. The reader may be relieved to hear that the Sandboys did eventually find tolerable quarters out at Wimbledon. As well as the special problems of his family, Mayhew describes the general scene during the weeks that preceded the opening:

'London, for some time previous to the opening of the Great Exhibition, had been a curious sight even to Londoners. All seemed to be preparing for the great fair – the world's holiday . . . In all the main thoroughfares, especially those leading from the railways and the docks, heavy vans, piled high with unwieldy packing-cases, or laden with some cumbrous machine, and drawn by a long team of horses, crawled along, creaking, on their way towards the Crystal Palace. The greater part of the principal streets were being repaired, preparatory to the increased traffic; shops were being newly painted . . . In almost every omnibus, some two or three foreigners were to be seen among the passengers, – either some light-haired Germans, or high-cheeked Americans, or sallow Turks, with their "fez-caps" of scarlet cloth . . . The road to the Crystal Palace had for a long time been an extraordinary scene. Extensive trains of waggons stretched far away, like an Eastern caravan, each waiting for its turn to be unloaded, monopolised one side of the carriage-way. Omnibuses, with their roofs crowded with people, went dashing by, while carts laden with building materials crept leisurely along . . . At almost every one of the public-houses some huge flag

21.   *Part of Richard Doyle's procession of visitors to the Exhibition.*

was flying from the upper windows . . . Along the edge of the footpath stood hawkers, shouting out the attractions of their wares – some had trays filled with bright silvery-looking medals of the Exhibition – others, pictures of it printed in gold on "gelatine-cards" – while others had merely barrows of nuts, baskets of oranges or trucks of the omni-present penny ginger-beer. Groups of foreigners, their beards yellow with dust, walked along with their hands stuck in their pockets, so as to make their full pantaloons even fuller than ordinary . . . Along Rotten Row, endless troops of equestrians galloped noiselessly along on the soft loose ground at the rear of the Crystal Palace – in front of it an interminable line of carriages crawled slowly past . . . On every side were mobs of spectators pressing close up to the rails, and standing on tip-toe, with their necks out-stretched, in the hope of getting a peep of what was going on within. All along the building were ladders, one beside each of the columns, with painters perched high upon them, busy colouring the iron-work against the opening day. On top of the huge glass arch that formed the roof of the transept, the tiny figures of workmen were to be seen, some walking along the crystal covering, and making one wonder how the fragile substance bore them. At the end of the building were steam-engines puffing out their white clouds of steam, and amid the *debris* of a thousand packing-cases stood giant blocks of granite, mammoth lumps of coal, stupendous anchors, and such huge articles as were too bulky to be placed within the building itself.

'All was bustle, life, confusion, and amazement.'

22.   *Part of Richard Doyle's procession of visitors to the Exhibition.*

23.　*Her Majesty's retiring room at the Crystal Palace. "The World's Metropolis".*

A TEMPLE MADE OF GLASS

THREE men were responsible for the conception and wild success of the Great Exhibition of the Works of Industry of All Nations: Prince Albert, Henry Cole and Joseph Paxton. All were individuals of exceptional ability and indomitable energy, yet of the three neither the prince, who was both a highly educated aesthete and an intelligent reformer, nor Cole, who was extraordinarily versatile and boundlessly enthusiastic, have received the honour due to them from posterity. Whether it was Albert or Cole who first conceived the idea of the Exhibition is moot. The fact is that they both ardently wanted to improve general taste which was recognized as being at a low level in England in spite of the small efforts of the governmental School of Design; they wanted to 'wed high art with mechanical skill' by means of official encouragement. That they failed in this was not for lack of trying. In the promotion of the Great Exhibition they both worked without reserve for its success and they co-operated famously together, being well acquainted through their meetings at the Royal Society of Arts – or the Society for the Encouragement of Arts, Manufactures and Commerce to give its full, explicit title – of which the prince had become President in 1845. Cole's genuine admiration of Albert is evident in his autobiography, *Fifty Years of Public Work* (1884): 'A prince of pre-eminent wisdom, of philosophic mind, sagacity, with power of generalship and great practical ability, placed himself at the head of the enterprise, and led it to triumphant success.'

It was at the Society of Arts that the idea of the Great Exhibition germinated, and although the Society had helped to mount three small shows of Art Manufactures in 1847, '48 and '49 under Cole's direction, nothing comparable in scope had been proposed before.

The gifted Cole, like Edwin Chadwick of the Board of Health, was before his time in his faith in bureaucratic leadership; he was therefore not popular in political circles and, like Chadwick, did not receive his accolade until late in life. His career began as Assistant Keeper at the Record Office, which he reformed; he helped Rowland Hill to establish the Penny Post, fought for the standard railway gauge and cheap rates for railway parcels, assisted in the establishment of the docks at Grimsby, reformed the Patent Laws, edited the *Journal of Design*, as 'Felix Summerly' was an industrial designer of merit (winning the Royal Society's silver medal in 1845 for a Minton tea service that sold abundantly and was popular for years), made the country conscious of Art Manufactures (to use his own term), pioneered technical education, built up the Victoria and Albert Museum, wrote books for children and books on art, published the first Christmas card (with a design by Maclise), and was a music critic and an accomplished painter and etcher in his own right.

Joseph Paxton was one of those remarkable individuals produced by the age of *laissez-faire* opportunity: self-made,

24. *Henry Cole. I.L.N. July 1873.*

self-educated, ambitious and bold. His life raises one of the minor mysteries of history: Why did not Samuel Smiles, who wrote *Self-Help* and *The Lives of the Engineers*, write the life of Paxton? His was the greatest success story of all time.

The son of a small Bedfordshire farmer, Paxton was born in 1801 and so lived perfectly poised in time between two ages – that of the landed aristocrats and that of the industrial capitalists – between the two worlds of Victorian England: etherial romanticism and earthy materialism. When working as under-gardener for the Horticultural Society at Chiswick, he was noticed by the sixth Duke of Devonshire and at the early age of twenty-three became head-gardener at Chatsworth. There he proceeded, with the duke's constant encouragement, to recreate the gardens and to erect fountains, cascades, arboreta, vineries, shrubberies, and glass-houses filled with exotic plants. His major work at Chatsworth was the Great Conservatory covering an acre of ground through which a carriage and pair could be driven. Before long he was managing the duke's other estates at Chiswick, Devonshire House, Hardwick, Lismore and Bolton Abbey, and was designing and building for his admiring patron not only glass-houses but a good deal of solid architecture of a somewhat clumsy Italianate sort that included the complete model village of Edensor. With the energetic support of his loving wife Sarah, he became not only the most famous gardener in the world, but made a fortune in railway shares, became a railway director, founded the *Daily News*, wrote books on and edited magazines devoted to horticulture, and, one year, made the Grand Tour with the duke to whom he became a constant, loyal but never sycophantic companion and adviser; as the duke was to declare, 'To me a friend, if ever man had one.' Finally, in his last years between 1854 and 1865, when he died at Sydenham, Paxton represented Coventry in Parliament.

By the time he created the Crystal Palace he was a wealthy man. He had been designing glass structures for over twenty years, so that his technical knowledge was practical and thorough. After the Crystal Palace he continued to design ferro-vitreous buildings of a monumental sort, but they were mostly unrealized projects: one for the New York Exhibition competition in 1851, the French Crystal Palace for St Cloud with three magnificent domes, the Crystal Sanatorium for the London Chest Hospital near Victoria Park, and that magnificent communication for London called the 'Great Victorian Way or Grand Girdle Railway and Boulevard under Glass' submitted to the Select Committee on Metropolitan Communications of 1855.

The legitimate father of the Crystal Palace was the Lily House he built at Chatsworth in 1849 to protect the giant Victoria Regia, a rare and freshly discovered tropical water plant, a seed of which had been brought to Kew from British Guiana in 1847. At Kew it did not flourish, but it did do so under Paxton's care in its new home at Chatsworth. When Paxton procured his seedling, its leaves were less than six inches in diameter; within three months, in its special tank of moving water, they were over four feet, and a month later the plant flowered for the first time in England. The sophisticated, economic, airy structure of the Lily House, with its hollow cast-iron columns serving as rain-water pipes from the guttering, and the system of ridge-and-furrow roof lights he was to use at the Crystal

25. *Joseph Paxton.*
Contemporary steel engraving from a photograph.

Palace and which he patented, was inspired by the floating leaf of the lily itself with its ribby skeleton – a leaf strong enough, as Paxton demonstrated, to bear the weight of Annie, his seven-year-old daughter. The difficult problem of providing light, heat, ventilation and drainage for a specific purpose were here perfectly and logically solved.

A number of official industrial exhibitions of a purely national character had been organised in France, the first in 1798 and the last and greatest in 1849. In England, only a few local shows had been held in the manufacturing towns, while in 1845 a Free Trade Bazaar had been arranged in the Covent Garden Theatre. But the Great Exhibition was the largest of its kind ever held and it was the first to include the works of all nations. Let Henry Cole's introduction to the Official Catalogue of the Great Exhibition now take up the tale:

'To aid in carrying out their intention of holding a National Exhibition in the year 1851, the Council of the Society [of Arts] caused a report on the French Exposition, held in 1849, to be made to them and printed... Immediately after the termination of the session of 1849, the prince took the subject under his own personal superintendence... The minutes of the meeting of several members of the Royal Society of Arts, held at Buckingham Palace on the 30th June 1849, set forth as follows: –

' "His Royal Highness communicated his views regarding the formation of a Great Collection of Works of Industry and Art in London in 1851, for the purposes of exhibition, and of competition and encouragement. His Royal Highness considered that such Collection and Exhibition should consist of the following divisions: –

Raw Materials

Machinery and Mechanical Inventions
Manufactures
Sculpture and Plastic Art generally.

' "...Various sites were suggested as most suitable for the building; which it was settled must be, on the first occasion at least, a temporary one. The Government had offered the area of Somerset House... His Royal Highness pointed out the vacant ground in Hyde Park on the south side, parallel with, and between, the Kensington Drive and the ride commonly called Rotten Row, as affording advantages which few other places might be found to possess. Application for this site could be made to the Crown. *

' "It was a question whether this Exhibition should be exclusively limited to British industry. It was considered that, whilst it appears an error to fix any limitation to the production of machinery, science, and taste, which are of no country, but belong, as a whole, to the civilized world, particular advantage to British industry might be derived from placing it in fair competition with that of other nations.

' "It was further settled that, by offering very large premiums in money, sufficient inducement would be held out to the various manufacturers to produce works which, although they might not form a manufacture profitable in the general market, would, by the effort necessary for their accomplishment, permanently raise the powers of production, and improve the character of the manufacture itself.

' "It was settled that the best mode of carrying out the execution of these plans would be by means of a Royal

---

* The prince had first proposed Leicester Square as a site; what he sought was a position that 'admitted of good access to high and low, rich and poor; and that those who went down in omnibuses would have equal facilities of approach with those who went in their private carriages'.

Commission, of which His Royal Highness would be at the head." '

On 3 January 1850 the names of the twenty-seven Commissioners were announced and they included Lord John Russell (the Prime Minister), the Duke of Buccleuch, Sir Robert Peel, William Gladstone, engineer William Cubitt, architect Charles Barry, sculptor Richard Westmacott, free-trade advocate Richard Cobden, and Henry Labouchere, MP. Under the Commission an Executive Committee was formed which included Henry Cole, engineer Robert Stephenson and architect Matthew Digby Wyatt, who was appointed its Secretary. The Royal Commission then held its first meeting on 11 January 1850. Less than fifteen months later the Exhibition was opened. The way it happened remains an astonishing tale.

Subscriptions were raised from various sources, even down to collecting boxes (the Duke of Wellington heading the list of subscribers), and they included £75,000 from a number of towns and seaports in the Kingdom. A fund of £230,000 was then underwritten by a number of people, including most of the Commissioners, on the security of which the Bank of England issued the necessary loans. Cole pointed out:

'Assistance has only been sought from the Government when it was indispensable, as in correspondence with other countries, the provision of a site for the building, the organization of police, etc.; and wherever such assistance, when granted, would have entailed expense, the cost of it has been defrayed from the funds of the Exhibition.'

In January 1850 a Building Committee was formed consisting of Lords Buccleuch and Ellesmere, Charles Barry, William Cubitt, Robert Stephenson, Robert Cocke-

26. *Raising the ribs of the transept roof. I.L.N. Dec. 1850.*

rell, I.K. Brunel and T.L. Donaldson, with Cubitt as Chairman. They immediately staged an international competition for designs for the exhibition building, though without committing themselves to the acceptance of any entry. In April two hundred and forty-five designs were received, thirty-eight from foreigners, and were publicly exhibited, a number being of ferro-vitreous construction. The Committee turned them all down and, having picked the world's brains, proceeded to produce a design of their own which was offered to tender. Being designed by committee it was inevitably a compromising, hybrid monstrosity, a huge solid conglomerate requiring fifteen million bricks and dominated by a gigantic dome designed by Brunel which was two hundred feet in diameter – eleven feet more than that of St Peter's in Rome. It was very costly, it would have taken far too long to erect, and it was hideous. The design was met with the public scorn it deserved, and served as a strong weapon in the hands of the active opposition to the whole scheme.

That some fine old elms would have to be cut down on the proposed site in Hyde Park served as another weapon in the opposition's ordnance, and these became known as 'John Bull's Trees of Liberty'. Some doctors warned that the foreign invasion would spread plague and venereal diseases throughout the land, clergymen fulminated against the sin of pride, while *The Times*, working itself into a lather, warned that foreigners were renting houses near the Park for use as bawdy houses and that 'the whole of Hyde Park and of Kensington Gardens will be turned into a bivouac of all the vagabonds in London'. And Colonel Charles Sibthorpe continued to spit out hysterical vituperations in the House of Commons against 'one of the greatest frauds, greatest humbugs, greatest absurdities ever known . . . that accursed building erected to encourage the foreigner at the expense of the already grievously-distressed English artisan'.

The project seemed to be in jeopardy and Prince Albert was in despair. Then the miracle happened. Paxton told how at a banquet held in his honour at Derby which was reported in his own organ, the *Daily News*, on 7 August 1851:

'It was not until this war of words was raging with great fierceness that the thought occurred to me of making a design which would obviate all objections. Fortunately at this time I was erecting a house of peculiar construction, which I had designed for the growth of that most remarkable plant, the Victoria Regia; and it is to this plant and to this circumstance that the Crystal Palace owes its direct origin. Being in London and having to see Mr Ellis, the member for Leicester, on business connected with the Midland Railway, I sought him at the Houses of Parliament, and found him at a morning sitting in the new House of Commons, which was held there on that day for the purpose of testing its fitness for use. Sir Charles Wood was addressing the House; but not a word of what he said could be heard in the Speaker's gallery; upon which I observed to Mr Ellis that I feared they would make a mistake in constructing the Great Exhibition Building, and that I had some thoughts of sending in a design that would solve the difficulties complained of. After a little further conversation Mr Ellis went with me to the Board of Trade to see Lord Granville. We did not find his lordship within; but Mr Henry Cole, one of the executive committee, happened to be there.

'I went to No. 1 Old Palace Yard, and after conversing for some time with Mr Cole, I found that the building committee had advertised that the plans and specifications for contractors to tender to would be ready in about a fortnight, and I also heard that the specifications would contain a clause by which those who tendered might also tender for designs differing from the plan of the building committee. From this moment I decided that I would prepare plans for a glass structure, and the first thing I actually did was to go to Hyde Park and step over the ground to ascertain the extent in length and breadth on which the building was to stand.

'Having made an engagement to be at the floating of the third tube on the Britannia bridge*, I could not commence the plan till after my return; and it was at the Midland station in this town [Derby], in one of the committee rooms, that the first mark on paper was made of the Crystal Palace; and the most remarkable part connected with the Crystal Palace is that the blotting paper sketch indicates the principal features of the building as it now stands, as much as the most finished drawings that have been made since. In nine days from the time of making the blotting paper sketch, I found myself again at Derby, with a roll of plans under my arm on my way to London. These plans, five in number, had, with the exception of one, been prepared by me at Chatsworth; the one not prepared there had been made for me by Mr Barlow, the eminent engineer of the Midland Railway, who kindly gave me his valuable assistance in calculating the strength of the columns and girders. At the Midland station I had the good fortune to accidentally meet with Mr Robert Stephen-

* Stephenson's tubular railway viaduct across the Menai Straits.

son, who had come from Newcastle by the same train in which I was going to London. On our journey I showed the plans to Mr Stephenson of the design, and he promised to lay the plans before the Royal Commission on the following day, which promise he fulfilled.

'As Lord Brougham had said much in the House of Lords against a brick building being erected in Hyde Park, I waited upon his lordship and explained to him the nature of my plans. From that day Lord Brougham has never uttered a word against the Exhibition building, but on the contrary his lordship became my warmest supporter. I also showed the plans to Lord Granville before they went before the Royal Commissioners . . .

'After my design had been laid before the Royal Commissioners, and had been investigated by the building committee, and seen at Buckingham Palace by Her Majesty and Prince Albert, I took the plans to New-street, Spring Gardens, and had the good fortune to find Mr Fox at his office. Mr Fox was much pleased with the design, and at once agreed to go heartily into it. Mr Henderson (Mr Fox's partner) and Mr Robert Lucas Chance, the great glass maker at Birmingham, were telegraphed to be in London early on Monday, and after a long consultation my plans were sent to Birmingham for the purpose of having detailed estimates and drawings prepared. The Royal Commissioners were made aware of the fact of Messrs Fox and Henderson's intention to tender for my design, and Mr Cole went to Birmingham to counsel Messrs Fox and Henderson to tender for covering the ground in the exact roof marked out by the ground-plan prepared by the Building Committee. Mr Brunel also suggested that the interior columns should be placed 24 feet apart instead of 20, in order to suit the

Exhibition. During the preparation of these plans and estimates, Messrs Fox and Henderson came to Chatsworth to settle with me some of the more important details, and I went twice to Birmingham to see the progress of the plans and estimates.

'During the preparation of the plans Mr Henderson suggested the transept; to this I at first objected; I did so on these grounds – namely, that as the Exhibition was to be a fair competition of skill for all nations, I held it to be right and fair that each exhibitor should have an equal advantage as regards position – which they could not have with the introduction of the transept; another objection I entertained was that it could not stand in the centre of the building as the ground plan was then arranged; but the moment Mr Henderson said it would impart strength and solidity to the building I assented to its introduction.

'At length the day for sending in the tender came, but considerable delay took place before it was finally accepted. I have before stated that in order to get the tender in it was necessary the building should cover the exact space marked out by the building committee; but in conforming to this plan the transept was obliged to be put into one side of the building, for the purpose of avoiding the great trees which now stand within it, but which according to the tender sent in were to be an open court. At one of the meetings of the building committee it was suggested to them that the transept should include the great trees; but there appeared at first sight a good deal of difficulty in accomplishing this, as at the time all the roofing was designed to be flat. We promised to see what could be done before the next meeting of the committee. I went direct with Mr Fox to his office, and while he arranged the ground plan so as to bring the trees into the centre of the building, I was contriving how they could be covered. At length I hit upon the plan of covering the Transept with a circular roof, similar to that of the great conservatory at Chatsworth, and made a sketch of it, which was copied that night by one of the draughtsmen, in order that I might have it to show Mr Brunel, whom I had agreed to meet on the ground the next day.

'Before nine o'clock the next morning Mr Brunel called at Devonshire House and brought me the heights of all the great trees; in the note containing the measurements, Mr Brunel wrote thus: "I mean to try and win with our plan, but I have thought it right to give your beautiful plan all the advantages it is susceptible of". I then showed Mr Brunel the plan I had made the night before, for covering the trees, with which he was much pleased. I have been led into these minute details; first, to show that the circular roof of the transept was designed by myself, and not by Mr Barry, as currently reported; secondly, to show the kindness and liberality of Mr Brunel . . .

'As soon as my design had been accepted, it was decided by the Royal Commission to entrust the superintendence of its construction to Mr William Cubitt, the President of the Civil Engineers' Institution, and Messrs Fox and Henderson had, as contractors, to submit the detail drawings respecting the strength of the building for his approval.'

The 'ordinary gardener's boy', as the queen described Paxton in wonderment in her Exhibition Journal, had come a long way. The verbal facility he had acquired is as impressive as his evident astuteness in tactics. No wonder the Iron Duke, now warming his old bones in a nation-wide affection, remarked of him, 'I would have liked

27.   *View of the south side from near Prince's Gate. Lithograph by Brannan.*

28. *Cut crystal fountain by Messrs. F. and C. Osler.*
Catalogue II.

that man for one of my generals'. Among Paxton's man-œuvres was the publication of his provisional proposal in the *Illustrated London News* for 6 July 1850 even before it had been accepted by the Commission. The sketch shows the plain box-like structure with its long tiered roof but without its transept, and it reveals how great a visual improvement the arch provided to the whole conception. An additional gallery was also added to the final design. The courage – even if it was born of desperation – with which the prince and the Commissioners accepted Paxton's revolutionary project on 26 July and carried it through with such immense verve and efficiency was admirable. As Cole wrote:

'As soon as the decision was made, fresh working draw-ings had to be prepared, and every means taken for expedit-ing the works. These were carried out under the super-intendence of Mr Cubitt, assisted by Mr D. Wyatt, Mr O. Jones, and Mr C. Wild. The formal deed of contract was not signed until the 31 October, although the first iron column was fixed as early as the 26 September 1850, the contractors having thereby incurred, in their preparations, a liability of £50,000 without any positive contract; in fact, great reciprocal confidence was manifested by the contracting parties . . . A deed of covenant, to remove the building and give up the site within seven months after the close of the Exhibition, namely before the 1 June, 1852, has been entered into between Her Majesty and the Com-missioners . . .

'At a very early period the Commissioners resolved that the whole space of any building should be equally divided, and that one-half should be offered to Foreign countries, and the other reserved to Great Britain and her colonies.'

29.　*Prince Albert painted on Sèvres porcelain. Tallis I.*

30.　*Queen Victoria painted on Sèvres porcelain. Tallis I.*

During August and September of 1850 the ground was levelled and the concrete foundations were laid together with thirty-four miles of iron pipes running through base-plates to take the hollow iron columns that were to be bolted to them, each eight inches in diameter, foundations which are still there today somewhere beneath the football pitches. The drain pipes would carry away the rain that would fall on the eighteen acres of glass roofing, run along the patent guttering and thence down the hollow supporting columns. The work gathered momentum and erection of the main fabric was accomplished at incredible speed without any scaffolding but only with the use of blocks, pulleys, masts, shear-legs and ropes. The initial force of thirty-nine men employed in September had grown by December to one of more than two thousand, most of them being paid twenty-five shillings a week (£1.25). As Paxton himself observed on one of his visits to the site, three columns and two girders were being erected in only sixteen minutes.

The phenomenal speed of erection was accomplished by dry construction, by use of standardized, interchangeable, mass-produced components, use of steam-driven machines, division of labour and general rationalization. The previous generation could not possibly have achieved the feat; the technical means were then not yet available, nor was the railway transport, nor the electric telegraph which could speed verbal communications and instructions. Machines on the site cut the sash bars and gutters into correct lengths, while seventy-six ingenious trolleys, that could be arched over with canvas against the weather, ran along the grooves of the gutters whereon two glaziers sat as they slid the glass panels into place. By this means

31. *Waiting for the Queen. Dickinson.*

32. *The Inauguration. Dickinson.*

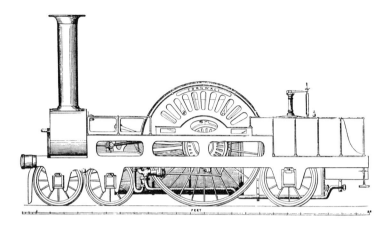

34. *Crampton's patent express engine, L.N.W.R. Catalogue I.*

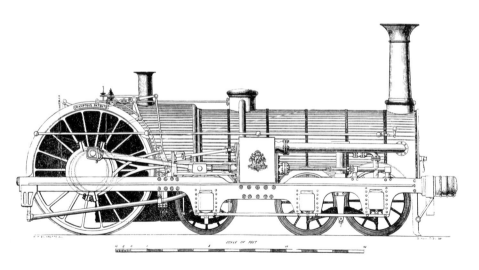

33. *The "Cornwall" express narrow-gauge engine, L.N.W.R. Catalogue I.*

eighty men could fix over eighteen thousand panes – some 63,000 square feet – in a week. As the framework proceeded, the sheet glass panels, each ten inches wide by forty-nine inches long – the largest that had yet been manufactured – were thus fixcd in place with putty, amounting in the end to 900,000 square feet of area, weighing some four hundred tons, and all supplied by the single firm of Chance Brothers of Smethwick, who had to import foreign labour to finish the contract on time.

To complete the framework, 1,060 iron columns were raised, many of them twenty feet long, bolted at the junctions. These supported 2,224 trellis girders, 358 trusses (amounting together to 550 tons of wrought iron and 3,500 tons of cast), thirty miles of Paxton guttering, 202 miles of sash bar. A remarkable amount of timber was used, amounting in all to 600,000 cubic feet. Early in December the great semi-circular ribs of laminated timber of the transept arch were raised and within a week all sixteen were in position. Much walling at ground floor was of vertical boarding in which ventilating louvres were fixed, while the flooring was all of timber boards set half an inch apart on timber joists to provide spaces through which the dust could be swept with machines at the end of each day. Glazing bars and guttering were also of wood, while eventually the eleven miles of stalls, to be covered with red cloth and pink calico, were all joiners' work. The structure was therefore by no means fire-proof.

On the north-west of the main building a boiler-house was built in matching style for generating the steam, supplied through underground pipes, required for the moving machinery. The smaller structure also contained a water tank to supply a main pipe running around the entire main building and joined centrally down the transept from which branch pipes ran to supply water not only to the several fountains but to a multitude of fire-cocks.

The whole structure was the first major example of modular construction, composed of standard parts that could be rapidly assembled and as rapidly dismounted, the standard unit of measurement – or module as we would call it – being throughout, both on the horizontal and vertical plane, twenty-four feet. Here was an entirely logical, functional solution to the problem of quickly providing a temporary enclosure for the public display of objects of every kind and size. Everything was thought out. With a typical eye for the dramatic, Dickens wrote in *Household Words*:

'Two parties in London relying on the accuracy and goodwill of a single ironmaster, the owners of a single glass-works in Birmingham and of one master-carpenter in London, bound themselves for a certain sum of money, and in a few months, to cover eighteen acres with a building upwards of a third of a mile long.'

As the structure rose glittering above the surrounding hoarding (finally to be re-used for the flooring), crowds gathered each day to watch the progress; on 25 February 1851 the number of watchers was estimated at over 100,000. Five shillings (25p) was eventually charged for admission to the site itself by the contractors, who placed the proceeds in an accident fund.

Five hundred painters followed the glaziers, and the results of their labours added to the attraction of the huge structure, for the colours were admirably chosen by the architect and decorator Owen Jones. The exterior was stone picked out with pale blue; inside, warm white covered

35. *Applegarth's vertical printing machine. Tallis II.*

the glazing bars, light blue the girders in general with red for their undersides, and yellow and blue the columns, while streamers of turkey red backed the railings or hung here and there from the girders. Finally, unbleached calico was suspended between the roof ridges and on the south side to reduce the sun's glare and heat. Tallis described the interior scene as the work proceeded:

'It would be difficult to describe the effect produced upon the minds of the spectators, when they found themselves within the structure, of which every point was still in progress. All manner of operations seemed going on at once; sawing, planing, glazing, painting, hammering, boarding. Here white vapours curled among the yet leafless branches of the imprisoned elms, from little steam-engines, each steadily fixed from day to day at its appointed duties. There clouds of dust covered the too curious spectator, from circular-saws, busily employed in cutting to equal

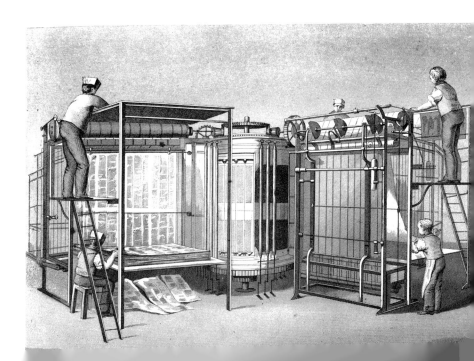

lengths, the Paxton gutters. Then again were machines kindly guiding those same gutters, first through a trough of paint, and then through an aperture provided with brushes, which pressing closely upon them, in their passage, turned them out of it at the other side, all trimly coated. One vast apparatus was busying itself with the making of putty; another with manufacturing sash-bars – here were vast boilers to generate steam for the machinery – there pipes diverging east and west, to convey to the fountains, and various parts of the building, the three hundred thousand gallons of water supplied per diem, by the Chelsea Waterworks Company, by contract, at fifty pounds per month. Massive cranes were relieving ponderous waggons of their loads, and wheels and pulleys were everywhere in motion.'

The job was completed on time. It had been magnificently organized. From the removal of the first sod to the last lick of paint, the whole enormous enterprise was accomplished in less than nine months. Thackeray was moved to versify:

'But yesterday a naked sod
The dandies sneered from Rotten Row
And cantered o'er it to and fro;
And see 'tis done!
As though 'twere by a wizard's rod
A blazing arch of lucid glass
Leaps like a fountain from the grass
To meet the sun!'

The great exhalation, 1848 feet long and 408 feet wide with its central transept 72 feet wide and rising to 108 feet, covered over eighteen acres of ground and enclosed thirty-three million cubic feet of space. Its galleries ran for nearly a mile and these added another five acres to the floor area. The main entrance was on the south side facing the Prince of Wales's Gate, but there were two other entrances and about seventeen exits. Ten wide staircases led to the galleries, and across the nave and aisles bridges joined the galleries to one another, so forming a series of courts holding ensembles that could be seen as entities from above.

Protests petered out. Everyone was thrilled by the effulgent apparition. And then *Punch*, which had been showing a certain amount of scepticism, produced the hallmark of success, through the pen of Douglas Jerrold, with an inspired title: THE CRYSTAL PALACE. *The Times* changed its tone:

'The vast fabric may be seen, by any one who visits that part of the town, in its full dimensions – an Arabian Night's structure, full of light, and with a certain airy unsubstantial character about it, which belongs more to an enchanted land than to this gross material world of ours. The eye, accustomed to the solid heavy details of stone and lime, or brick-and-mortar architecture, wanders along those extended and transparent aisles, with their terraced outlines, almost distrusting its own conclusions on the reality of what it sees, for the whole looks like a splendid phantasm, which the heat of the noon-day sun would dissolve, or a gust of wind scatter into fragments, or a London fog utterly extinguish . . . Everything is done by the rule, and yet everything is graceful, and it might almost be said grand . . . and it is certainly curious to reflect, now that the work has been accomplished, and the great result stands patent to the world, that, with the facilities we possessed, glass and iron have hitherto been

36. Great Exhibition exterior – raw materials. Dickinson.

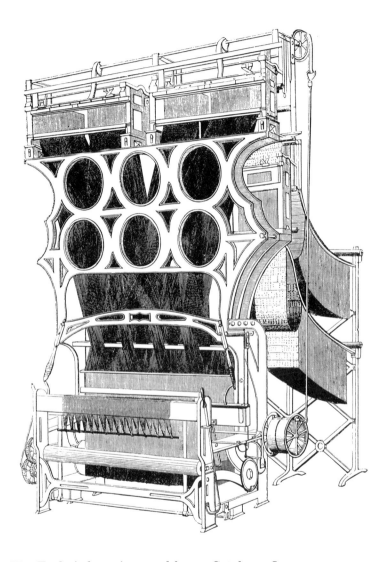

37. Taylor's large jacquard loom. Catalogue I.

so little employed by our architects.'

As the novel structure neared completion first a stream and then a torrent of 100,000 objects arrived from the 5,000 exhibitors and were channelled with masterly organization into their allotted places. One of the numerous crates arrived safely from France carefully labelled: 'To Sir Vyatt and Sir Fox Enderson Esquire, Grate Exposition Park of Hide at London. GLACE SOFTLY TO BE POSED UPRIGHT'. Only part of the Russian consignment failed to arrive on time due to ice in the Baltic.

The opening ceremony took place as planned on the first of May, a genial but showery day. By eleven o'clock well over half a million people had assembled in the Park, all eyes turned towards the gaily coloured ranges of the flags of all nations that fluttered along the roofs of the gleaming structure. The model frigate *Prince of Wales* floated on the Serpentine, its crew at the ready to fire a salute, while Mr Charles Spencer, the celebrated aeronaut, stood beside his basket ready to ascend in his balloon at the instant the Exhibition was declared open. Mayhew described the London scene of that memorable day:

'The morning was ushered in with merry peals from almost every steeple; afar off the drone of the thousand bells sounded like the boom of a huge gong – the signal, as it were, for the swarming of the Great Hive . . . With the first gleam of daylight, the boys of London, ever foremost at a sight, had taken up their places in the trees, like their impudent counterparts, the London sparrows, and men and women grouped round the rails, determined at least to have a good place for seeing the opening of the World's Show. Hammers were to be heard on all sides, fastening the timbers of the wooden stages that were being set up by the many who delight in holidays solely as a matter of business. Some were pouring in at the Park gates, laden with tables and chairs for the sight-seers to stand upon. Others again came with the omnipresent street provisions – huge trucks filled with bottles of ginger beer – baskets of gingerbread and "fatty cakes" – and tins of brandy-balls and hardbakes–while from every quarter there streamed girls and women with round wicker sieves piled up in pyramids with oranges. Then there were the women with the brown-looking trotters, spread on white cloths, and the men with their ham sandwiches, as thin as if made out of whitey-brown paper; while at the gates, and all along the roads, stood men with trays of bright silvery looking medals of the Crystal Palace, and filling the air with the cheapness and attractions of their wares . . .

'As the morning advanced the crowds that came straggling on, grew denser and denser, till at last it was one compact kind of road, paved with heads; and on they went – fathers with their wives and children, skipping jauntily along, and youths with their gaily-dressed sweet-hearts, in lively-coloured shawls and ribbons – and many, early as it was, munching apples, or cracking nuts as they trudged on their way. All London, and half the country, and a good part of the world, were wending their way to see the Queen pass in state to open the GREAT EXHIBITION OF ALL NATIONS.'

By midday a thousand carriages of state had passed through the park gates together with two and a half thousand other cabs and vehicles. Some 30,000 privileged people were at last assembled under the glass roof of the Palace where the great elms, forming a perfect organic foil to the geometry of the structure, were already sprouting

38. *Heckmann's vacuum boiling apparatus from Russia. Catalogue III.*

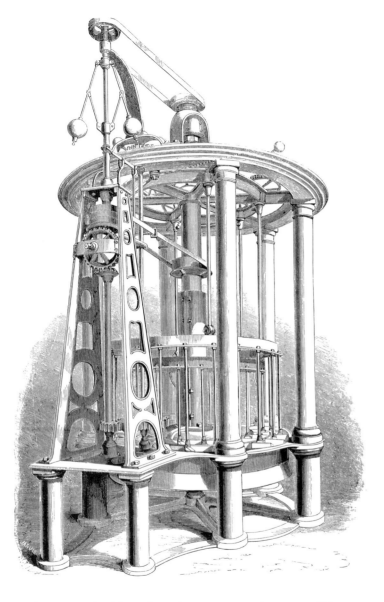

39. *Improved double turbine from France. Catalogue III.*

their spring greenery. Among those waiting inside was Mayhew:

'A kind of coloured rainbowy air appeared to pervade the whole building, while, as the eye travelled down the long vista of galleries, and beheld the forms and tints at the end of the avenues, dimmed by the haze of distance, one was struck with a solemn sense of the majesty of the building ... There was the canopy above the royal seat, and adorned with its golden cornice and fringe, and with a small plume of blue and white feathers at each of the angles. The floors were no longer strewn, but clean and matted, and at each corner of the central square, stages had been raised for the most illustrious visitors ... From the top of the galleries were hung huge carpets and pieces of tapestry, gorgeous in their tints, and exquisite in their designs ... At every corner were statues, made doubly white by the scarlet drapery arranged behind them, while immediately at the back of the throne were two equestrian statues of the Prince and Queen, one on either side ... But it was when the retinue of the court began to assemble that the scene became one – perhaps the most gorgeous in colouring and splendour ever beheld; for it was seen in the clear light of the transparent roof above. The gold embroidered bosoms of the officers of State seemed to be almost alight with the glitter of their ornaments; and as the ambassadors of all nations stood grouped in the centre, the various forms and colours and embellishments of their costumes were a sight to see and never to forget ... There was the turbanded Turk, and the red fez-capped Egyptian; and there were the chocolate-coloured court suits, with their filagree steel buttons, and long, white, embroidered silk waistcoats. There was the old Duke, too, with his

40. *Moving machinery. Dickinson.*

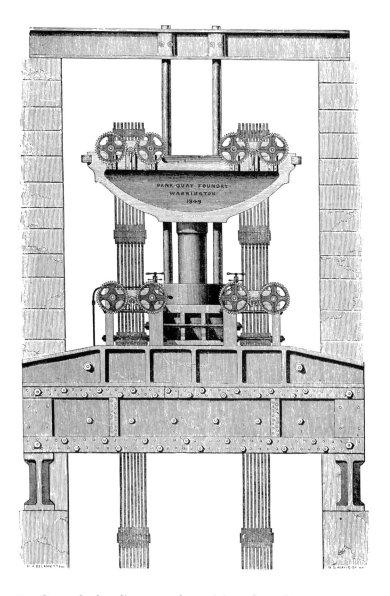

silver hair and crooked back showing most conspicuous amongst the whole. At the back and sides of the throne, stood the gentlemen at-arms, in their golden helmets, with the long plumes of the white ribbon-like feathers drooping over them. Beside these were the portly-looking beef-eaters, in their red suits and black velvet caps, and near them were the trumpeters, in their golden coats and close-fitting jockey-caps, with silver trumpets in their hands. Near these were the Aldermen, in their red gowns of office, trimmed with fur; and the Common-councilmen, in their blue silk gowns; and the Recorder, in long, big, powdered judge's wig – the Archbishop, in full lawn sleeves, and close, curly wig – and the 'Musical Doctor', in his white satin, damask robe, and quaint-looking cap – and the heralds in their blue silk robes, emblazoned with gold-looking lions, and other silken devices – and the Garter King-at-Arms, in his gorgeous red velvet coat, becrested all over with gold – while, round all these, were ranged sappers and miners, in their red and yellow uniforms; and behind them were seen the dark blue coats of the police. It was a feast of colour and splendour to sit and gloat over . . .

'At a few minutes before the appointed hour, the royal carriages with their bright liveries were seen to flash past the windows of the northern entrance – then darted by a troop of Life Guards, with their steel helmets and breast-plates glistening in the sunshine, and immediately after, the glass sides and roof of the Crystal Palace twanged with the flourish of trumpets, that announced the arrival of the Queen.'

The queen, accompanied by Prince Albert (not yet 'Consort'), the Prince of Wales and the Princess Royal,

41. *Great hydraulic press for raising the tubes of the Britannia Railway Bridge. Catalogue I.*

entered the retiring room. The queen wore a dress of pink satin sparkling with diamonds and silver and crowned with a tiara of diamonds and feathers; Prince Albert was in a field-marshal's uniform, the young Prince of Wales in Highland dress and the princess in white lace with a wreath of wild roses in her hair. A burst of cheering greeted the approach of the royal party; the bronze gates guarded by Beefeaters were thrown open, the party proceeded to the dais and the National Anthem was sung; prayers, speeches, singing and blasts from young Henry Willis's Grand Organ were followed by a tour of inspection headed by Paxton and Fox, return to the dais and a declaration by Lord Bredalbane to the assembly that the Exhibition was open. Trumpetings and the boom of cannon without concluded the impressive kind of ceremony at which the nation has always been adept.

The general excitement of the occasion was intense and hinted at an almost religious fervour. The queen herself was 'filled with devotion'; the building seemed to be a great fane, its nave and its transept harbouring an impressive ritual, like that of some cathedral service, to open the show to the accompaniment of holy blasts from the organ, trumpetings and swelling choruses of Hallelujahs, and an interminable prayer uttered by the Archbishop of Canterbury. The Deity was clearly on the side of expanding markets, bulbous decoration, *Pax Britannica* and, perhaps also, to quote *Punch*'s terrible pun, of *Paxton Vobiscum*.

That night the queen confided to her Exhibition Journal: 'This is one of the greatest and most glorious days of our lives, with which, to my pride and joy, the name of my dearly beloved Albert is for ever associated! ... The Park presented a wonderful spectacle, crowds streaming through it, – carriages and troops passing, quite like the Coronation, and for *me*, the same anxiety. The day was bright and all bustle and excitement. At ½p II the whole procession in 9 State carriages was set in motion, Vicky and Bertie were in our carriage (the other children and Vivi did not go). The Green Park and Hyde Park were one mass of densely crowded human beings, in the highest good humour and most enthusiastic. I never saw Hyde Park look as it did, being filled with crowds as far as the eye could reach. A little rain fell, just as we started, but before we neared the Crystal Palace, the sun shone and gleamed upon the gigantic edifice, upon which the flags

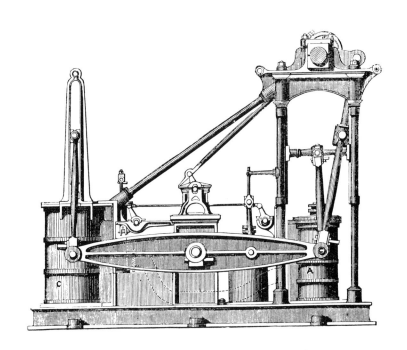

42. *McNaught's patent double cylinder steam-engine. Catalogue I.*

of every nation were flying . . . The sight as we came to the centre where the steps and chair (on which I did *not* sit) was placed, facing the beautiful crystal fountain was magic and impressive. The tremendous cheering, the joy expressed in every face, the vastness of the building, with all its decorations and exhibits, the sound of the organ (with 200 instruments and 600 voices, which seemed nothing) and my beloved husband, the creator of this peace festival "uniting the industry and art of all nations of the earth", all this was indeed moving, and a day to live for ever'.

'Quite satisfactory', declared Prince Albert. The rest of the country agreed with acclaim and began to show more respect for the prince in spite of his foreign accent and the *hauteur* that was the product of shyness. 'I never remember anything before', Lord Aberdeen was to tell the queen, 'that *everyone* was pleased with, as is the case with this Exhibition'.

Tennyson wrote a paeon of praise, and an old and apposite dream of Chaucer's from his *House of Fame* was often quoted. It is as curiously prescient as that seeming prophesy of an RAF squadron in flight to be found in Chapter I of *Ezekiel*. Its mellifluence alone requires a reprint here:

'I dreamt I was
Within a temple made of glass,
In which there were more images
Of gold, standing in sundry stages,
In more rich tabernacles
And with jewels, more pinnacles,
And more curious portraitures,
And quaint manner of figures
Of gold-work than I saw ever.

Then saw I stand on either side,
Straight down to the doors wide
From the dais many a pillar
Of metal that shone out full clear.

Then gan I look about and see
That there came ent'ring in the hall
A right great company withal,
And that of sundry regions,
Of all kinds of conditions
That dwell on earth beneath the moon,
Poor and rich.

Such a great congregation
Of folks as I saw roam about,
Some within and some without,
Was never seen nor shall be more.'

For the first week or two, wrote Mayhew, 'the road within a mile of the Glass Hive was blocked with carriages. From the Prince of Wales's Gate to Apsley House there stretched one long line of cabs, omnibuses, carriages, broughams, flies, now moving for a few minutes, and now stopping for double the time, while the impatient visitors within let down the blinds and thrust out their heads see how far the line extended. At every intersecting thoroughfare stood clusters of busy policemen, seizing horses by the reins, and detaining the vehicles till the cross current had in a measure ceased. And here might be seen persons threading between the blocked carriages, and bobbing beneath the horses' heads, in order to pass from one side of the road to the other. To seek to pass through the Park gates was

43. Printing and envelope folding machine on the stand of Thomas de la Rue and Company. Lloyd.

44. *Holmes of Derby: Light park phaeton. "Art Journal".*

45. *Mulliner's "Pilentum". "Art Journal".*

about as dangerous an experiment as "shooting" the centre arch of Old London Bridge.'

The carriage folk were allowed in first, for on the second and third days the admission price was £1, and from the fourth day up to the twenty-first day it was five shillings (25p). Thereafter it was reduced to a shilling (5p) from Mondays to Thursdays, half-crown (12½p) on Fridays, and five shillings again on Saturdays. To avoid delays, no change was given at the doors. Season tickets, of which 25,000 were sold, were available at three guineas for gentlemen and two for ladies, and these gave admission to the opening ceremony.

Saturday mornings were reserved for invalids until noon. 'There are many real invalids', wrote Tallis, 'but there are also some false ones, who, as soon as they have obtained admission, like Sixtus Quintus, get rid of their crutches, a circumstance which gives the Crystal Palace a certain likeness to the Court of Miracles.' Drinking of alcohol, smoking and the company of dogs were prohibited within the building, and there was no Sunday opening.

At first the shilling visitors tended to stay away, but soon, as the word got around, they came in ever-growing numbers so that in the end the influx outstripped the expectations of even the most sanguine of the organizers. Towards the end of the Exhibition *The Times* was to report (13 October), 'The greatest number of people ascertained to have been in the building at any one time, was at 2 o'clock on Tuesday last, when 92,000 persons were present.'

On the cheap days, parishes arrived headed by their vicar, soldiers by their colonels, sailors by their captains, and school children by their ushers. To quote Mayhew again:

'Here you see a railway guard, with the silver lettering on his collar, and his japan pouch by his side hurrying towards the locomotive department. Next, you come to a carpenter, in his yellow fluffy flannel jacket, descanting on the beauties of a huge top, formed of one section of a mahogany tree. Then may be seen a hatless and yellow-legged Blue-coat boy mounting the steps of one of the huge prismatic lighthouses . . . Peeping into the model of the Italian Opera are several short-red-bodied and long-black-legged Life Guardsmen; while, among the agricultural instruments, saunter clusters of countrymen in smock-frocks. On the steps of the crimson-covered pedestals are seated small groups of tired women and children, some munching thick slices of bread and meat, the edges of which are yellow with oozing mustard . . . The machinery, which has been from the first the grand focus of attention, is, on the shilling days, the most peculiar sight of the whole. Here every other man you rub against is habited in a corduroy jacket, or a blouse, or leathern gaiters . . . You see the farmers, their dusty hats telling of the distance they have come, with their mouths agape, leaning over the bars to see the self-acting mills at work . . . But the chief centres of curiosity are the power-looms, and in front of these are gathered small groups of artisans, and labour-ers, and young men whose red coarse hands tell you they do something for their living, all eagerly listening to the attendant, as he explains the operations, after stopping the loom . . . At the steam brewery, crowds of men and women are continually ascending and descending the stairs; youths are watching the model carriages moving along the new pneumatic railway; young girls are waiting to see the hemi-spherical lamp-shades made out of a flat sheet of

46. *Hallmarke of London; park phaeton. " Art Journal".*

47. *Carriage by Clapp of Boston. " Art Journal".*

paper; indeed, whether it be the noisy flax-crushing machine, or the splashing centrifugal pump, or the clatter of the Jacquard lace machine, or the bewildering whirling of the cylindrical steam-press, – round each and all these are anxious, intelligent, and simple-minded artisans, and farmers, and servants, and youths, and children, clustered, endeavouring to solve the mystery of its complex operations.'

Before the shilling days began, the great topic of conversation and speculation was how the crowds would behave in the metropolis in general and at the Exhibition in particular. Would drunkenness prevail? Would crime increase? Would riots occur? If so, the Iron Duke, who sniffed trouble in every breeze and knew by direct experience how violently mobs could behave, had made ample preparations by dispersing 10,000 extra troops around the town and within the Park, while Richard Mayne, Chief Commissioner of Police, added a thousand men to the Metropolitan Force. As it turned out, everyone behaved with astonishing decorum. Within the Exhibition, among the six million visitors, supported by some fifty policemen in their toppers with truncheons at their sides, the public was its own protector. The number of offences charged during the months when the Exhibition was open, was no more than twenty-five – nine for picking pockets, six for attempting to do so, and ten for petty larceny at the stalls. No one died at the show and one child was born there. On her many visits the queen would wander around among the crowds without protection, comforting the smug that all was well with the country and its Constitution. As G.M. Young writes in his *Portrait of an Age*, 'The Great Exhibition was the pageant of domestic peace. Not for sixty years had the throne appeared so solidly based on the national goodwill as in that summer of hope and pride and reconciliation.'

Only light refreshments were sold in the building. Cole reports in his introduction to the Catalogue:

'The Commissioners considered that it would conduce to the convenience of visitors to permit light and moderate refreshments to be obtained and consumed *in certain prescribed parts* of the building but that it would be inconsistent with the nature of the Exhibition to allow the building to assume the character of an hotel, tavern, or dining-rooms. In the Central Area are sold ices, pastry, sandwiches, patties, fruits, tea, coffee, cocoa, lemonade, seltzer and soda water; whilst in the Eastern and Western

48. *Garrett's improved threshing machine. I.L.N. Aug. 1851.*

49. *Agricultural machinery by Garrett and Son. Lloyd.*

50. Ornamented console table and looking glass. Catalogue II.

Areas are sold bread, butter and cheese, tea, coffee, chocolate, cocoa, ginger beer, spruce beer, and similar drinks, together with the other articles sold to the visitors. The privilege of supplying refreshments on these terms was put up to competition, and the tender of Messrs Schweppe, wherein they offered a sum of £5,500 for the privilege, was accepted. Waiting rooms and conveniences have likewise been provided at a moderate charge at each of the refreshment areas.'

This was, in fact, the first time that public Comfort Stations had been provided anywhere; some were free, others were not, and the latter produced a profit of no less than £1,769. All prices at the buffets were fixed by the Committee and throughout the building were interspersed drinking fountains of filtered water. Though Cole does not mention this, plates of cold meat supported by steamed potatoes could also be had, but otherwise all cooking was prohibited. The ices available, which cost 6d and 1s (2½p and 5p), were made in a patent freezing machine run by steam on the spot. Buns, soda water, lemonade and ginger beer sold best, the grand total of buns consumed being 1,804,718. Schweppe's made a profit of £45,000.

Around the Crystal Palace, in the open, the exhibits consisted to some extent in objects which were too large or heavy to take inside, but mainly they were raw materials, including minerals and mining products, one item being a monster block of coal weighing twenty-four tons from the Duke of Devonshire's Stavely mines. Other items included blocks of granite, slate, stone and gypsum, a figure of Lazarus in artificial stone, granite obelisks, huge earthenware pots, life-boats, great naval anchors, hot-houses and

51.   *Furniture from Austria made of iron tubes. Catalogue III.*

52. *Fabrics. Lloyd.*

goods in its own way. At the centre of the crossing stood the famous Crystal Fountain Follett Osler had made specially for the Exhibition from four tons of pure crystal glass – a sparkling focus and useful point of rendezvous twenty-seven feet high that was to stand in the rebuilt Palace at Sydenham to the very end after eighty-five years of existence. Throughout the building, here and there, arose great organs that were played at intervals throughout the day, the grandest being that of Willis with its 45,000 pipes.

An important organizer of the exhibits was Dr Lyon Playfair, for he prepared the classifications, adapting in a practical way Prince Albert's four logical but far too rigid categories. He also superintended the awards of the international juries; he was, in short, chief liaison officer to the Exhibition. (His most valuable work followed the Exhibition, for he remained a member of the 1851 Commission for forty-five years, became Secretary of the Science and Art Department in 1855, and was for a while Liberal MP for the Scottish universities and then of South Leeds; in 1892 he was granted a peerage.)

At the Exhibition, Europe was represented by France (the largest foreign contributor), by Germany, Austria, Italy, Belgium, Denmark jointly with Sweden and Norway, Holland, Greece, Spain, Portugal, Russia, Switzerland and Turkey. The German area was sub-divided into the states of the Steuerversin, the two Mecklenburgs, the Hansa towns and the Zollverein, a common market of several states consisting of some twenty-six million people (*zoll* meaning customs duty). Italy was also sub-divided as Naples, Rome, Sardinia and Tuscany. The full national unities of Germany and Italy had not yet been achieved.

so on. Some way from the western end of the building rose the colossal equestrian statue of Richard Cœur de Lion by Baron Marochetti, which can be seen today beside the Houses of Parliament with sword aloft.

The whole of the western half of the Crystal Palace was occupied by the British exhibits, while foreign goods occupied the eastern half. Machinery lay right along the north side, while the statues were placed in the nave and along the centre of the transept. No objects of fine art were included and sculpture was accepted, ostensibly at least, only if it demonstrated some new or notable method of manufacture. Each nation was allowed to display its

53. *France. Dickinson.*

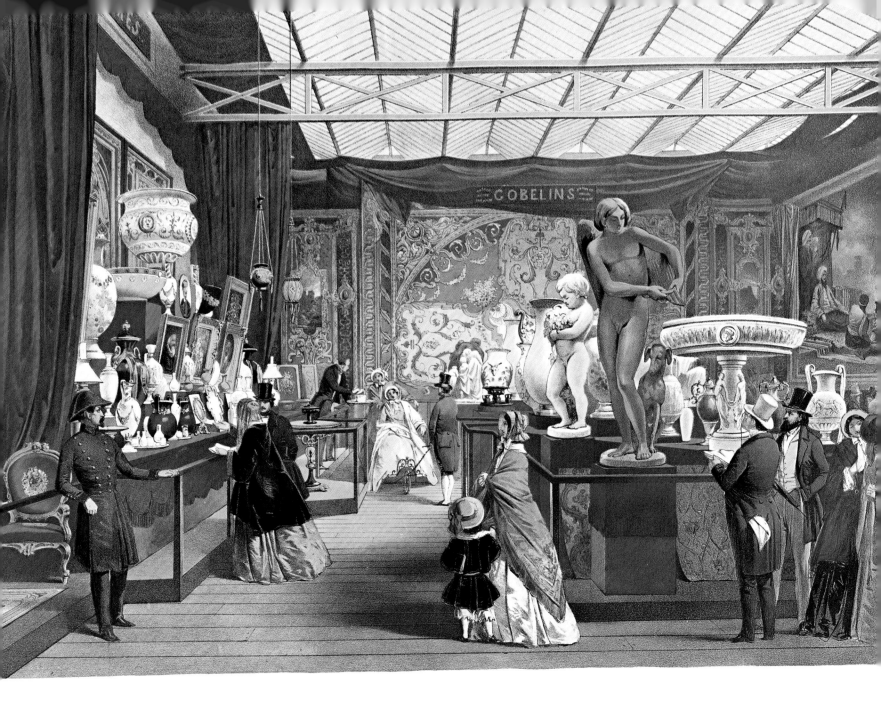

54. *Elephant and howdah from India. Catalogue II.*

From the Americas came Bolivia, Brazil, Buenos Aires, Chile, Ecuador, Mexico, Montevideo, New Granada, Peru, Venezuela and the United States. Other contributors were Arabia, Egypt, Morocco, Persia, Tunis and West Africa. China sent nothing herself but England was combed for Chinese items that would form a display.

Some 100,000 objects of every sort were exhibited along a total frontage of more than ten miles by over 15,000 contributors. They are all listed, described and sometimes illustrated in the three fat volumes of the official catalogue, and composed a fantastic riot of the practical and the ornate – of mechanisation and handicrafts – of elegance and vulgarity – of the useful and the ridiculous. The Machinery Courts drew the largest crowds and the queen visited these more frequently than any other section of the Exhibition. She wrote in her Journal:

'Went to the machinery part, where we remained two hours, and which is excessively interesting and instructive ... What used to be done by hand and used to take months doing is now accomplished in a few instants by the most beautiful machinery. We saw first the cotton machines, from Oldham ... Mr Whitworth's planing of iron tools, another for shearing and punching iron of just $\frac{1}{2}$ an inch thick, doing it as if it were bread! ... What was particularly interesting was a printing machine on the vertical principle, by which numbers of sheets are printed, dried and everything done in a second ... We saw hydraulic machines, pumps, filtering machines of all kinds, machines for purifying sugar, – in fact, every conceivable invention. We likewise saw medals made by machinery, which not more than 15 years ago were made by hand, 50 million instead of *one* million can be supplied

55. *Native musical instruments from India. Catalogue II.*

56. *American reaping machine by McCormick. I.L.N. July 1851.*

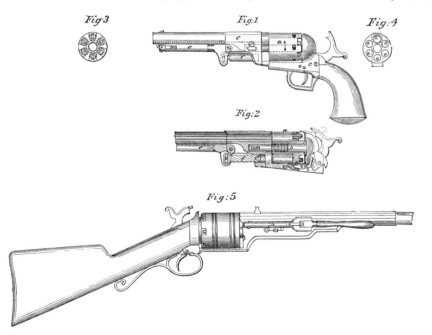

Fig:3   Fig:1   Fig:4

Fig:2

Fig:5

57. *Colt's repeating fire-arms. Catalogue III.*

in a week now . . . mills for grinding wheat and linseed, and for extracting oil from the latter. A large one, the largest in the Exhibition, invented by Mr S. Russell, for crushing sugar cane and extracting the juice, another for cleaning corn and grain; coffee mills; – a very curious machine for making chocolate; a very ingenious one for making cigarettes and wrapping them up in paper, – all done by the same machine . . . Went through the part with machinery, not in motion; consisting chiefly of locomotives, railway carriages of every kind and sort, . . . new modes of shifting carriages from one rail to another; . . . models of the first locomotives ever made and used in 1785, before railroads existed! the great hydraulic lever, or press, moved by one man with which the great Tubular Bridge at Bangor was raised, which is most wonderful. We next saw models of locomotion, amongst which one of a most ingenious contrivance for transferring mail bags on railways, going at full speed, the one being caught by a machine and dropped into a sort of net, while the other is taken up. We likewise saw another very clever patent soda water machine by which soda water can be made in incredibly short time merely with gas. . . We came home at 1/4 to 12, and I felt quite done and exhausted, *mentally* exhausted.'

The printing apparatus watched by the queen was Applegarth & Cowper's printing machine that churned out five thousand copies of the *Illustrated London News* every hour. The largest machine in the show was the steam press for raising the tubes, each weighing 1,144 tons, of Stephenson's tubular railway bridge that had so impressed the queen. A close second in size was James Nasmyth's steam-hammer that could be so perfectly adjusted that it could forge the massive main bearing of a steamship or gently crack an egg.

58. *America. Dickinson.*

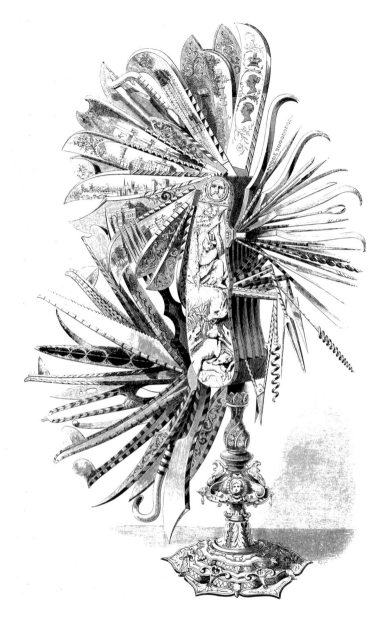

59. *Sportsman's Knife containing eighty blades and other instruments. Catalogue II.*

There was a beam engine in the Egyptian style, an oscillating engine embellished with Gothic tracery, an apparatus for supplying rooms and buildings with pure warm air, and many small machines, one for making envelopes, for example, and another for making knife handles. The agricultural machinery drew the country folk who were particularly impressed by McCormick's revolutionary reaping machine from the United States. Bolton and Watts steam engines were, of course, displayed (with many others) in motion. And there were models of all kinds – one of the Niagara Falls, a suspension bridge for a railway across the English Channel, a ship canal through the isthmus of Suez, the whole of Liverpool Docks, the new Britannia Tubular Railway across the Menai Straits, Stephenson's High-Level Bridge at Newcastle, Brunel's railway bridge at Chepstow, the Lord Mayor's State Barge, a steamer with feathering paddle wheels (a system which came to nothing for the screw propeller was on the way). One exhibitor showed the model of a carriage that supplied its own rails, a sort of Temporary Way, laying them down as it advanced and taking them up after the wheels and passed over them. Three examples of atmospheric railways running on compressed air were on display and several new adding machines, modest ancestors of the cybernetic revolution.

Textile machinery was, naturally, a major English contribution – for spinning and wool-combing, knitting, lace-making, ribbon embroidery, and hosiery. A notice from the *Giornale di Roma* gave a spirited account of one example:

'You stop before a small brass machine, about the size of a quart bottle; you fancy it is a meat-roaster: not at all. Ha! Ha! It is a tailor. Yes, a veritable *stitcher*. Present a

60. *Bright steel reflecting stove-grate in the Renaissance style. Catalogue II.*

piece of cloth to it: suddenly it becomes agitated, it twists about, screams audibly – a pair of scissors are projected forth – the cloth is cut; a needle sets to work, and lo and behold, the process of sewing goes on with a feverish activity, and before you have taken three steps, a pair of *inexpressibles* are thrown down at your feet, and the impatient machine, all fretting and fuming, seems to expect a second piece of cloth at your hands. Take care, however, as you pass along, that this most industrious of all possible machines does not lay hold of your cloak or great coat; if it touches even the hem of the garment, it is enough – it is appropriated, the scissors are whipped out, and with its accustomed intelligence the machine sets to work, and in the twinkling another pair is produced of that article of attire, for which the English have as yet been able to discover no name in their most comprehensive vocabulary.'

South of the machinery in motion lay the Carriage Court, and here, to our eyes at least, were shown the most elegant artifacts of the age – gleaming products of a craft that had reached the height of sophisticated skill: phaetons, gigs, broughams (pronounced brooms), cabriolets, coburgs, clarences, dog carts, sociales, richmonds, landaulets and omnibuses, with one or two velocipedes thrown in for good measure. Strangely enough no Patent Safety Cab, that Gondola of London, was included, although Joseph Aloysius Hansom, architect and founder of *The Builder* magazine, had invented it back in the thirties.

Another foreign visitor, a Frenchman, is also worth quoting from Tallis:

'England, as you are aware, reserved half the Crystal Palace for the exhibition of its own products . . . while the foreign nave is filled with *objects of art*, properly speaking, the English is principally occupied by *objects of utility* . . . The American exhibition is crowned, at the extremity of the nave, by an immense organ, the pipes of which are ornamented in such a manner, that they resemble great penny trumpets or gigantic sugar-sticks. From American to English art the transition is easy. Both are of the same character, generally prosaic . . . Wherever you find very beautiful silks, they are probably from Lyons . . . Sheffield cutlery, consisting of pen-knives with five or six hundred blades, two hundred and fifty pairs of scissors of every kind, one of the triumphs of England. Then enormous glasses; then light-houses and improved telescopes; then a trophy of furs, exhibited by the Hudson's Bay Company; then models of every kind.

'After this excursion in the nave of the Crystal Palace, let us go, if you please, to see the adoration of the relics.

61. *Pugin's Mediaeval Court. Dickinson.*

62. *Stained-glass Gallery. Dickinson.*

On the right, and nearly at the entrance to the foreign nave, you observe a crowd, curious and eager, flocking about a great parrot-cage with gilded bars. Within that is placed on a cushion the *Koh-i-Noor*. This diamond supplies, in the history of Central Asia, the place of the golden fleece, and has occasioned more than one bloody war. It ultimately came into the hands of Runjeet Singh, and when, after his death, England annexed his kingdom in its Indian possessions, the "Mountain of Light" was sent to London. It is now, if not the most curious, at least the most attractive article in the Exhibition. It weighs 186 carats. As to its value, it is necessarily nominal; it may be worth two millions, or nothing. To ordinary eyes it is nothing more than an egg-shaped lump of glass. They may show us what they please, and call it Koh-i-Noor. On ordinary days, that is, the shilling days, it is exposed in its great

cage, ornamented with a policeman, and they rely on the sun to cause it to sparkle; but on Friday and Saturday it puts on its best dress; it is arrayed in a tent of red cloth, and the interior is supplied with a dozen little jets of gas, which throw their light on the god of the temple. Unhappily, the Koh-i-Noor does not sparkle even then. Thus the most curious thing is not the divinity, but the worshippers . . . The Koh-i-Noor is well secured; it is placed on a machine which causes it, on the slightest touch, to enter an iron box. It is thus put to bed every evening, and does not get up till towards noon. The procession of the faithful then commences, and only finishes at seven o'clock . . .

'There is another thing, also, which has the same effect. It is a fountain of Eau de Cologne of Maria Farina. This is also guarded by a policeman, who takes quietly your handkerchief, passes it across a *jet d'eau*, and returns it perfumed.'

Novelties of the Exhibition included the largest sheet of plate glass ever made, the largest mirror in the world, an immense sheet of paper no less than 2,500 feet long, a table of inlaid wood mosaic containing two million pieces, a 'superior fertiliser' of bird droppings called guano, ground nuts from which oil could be extracted, a pharmaceutical product obtained from the livers of cod fish, phosphor matches, a 'window cleaner for the protection of female servants from fatal accidents and public exposure', a canister of boiled mutton supplied for an arctic expedition, which had been discovered in 1849, after twenty-five years, in a perfect state of preservation, an artificial silver nose, bleeding instruments as 'substitutes for leeches', 'tangible ink for the blind, producing raised characters on paper' (a precursor of Braille), a 'portable letter-case for taking

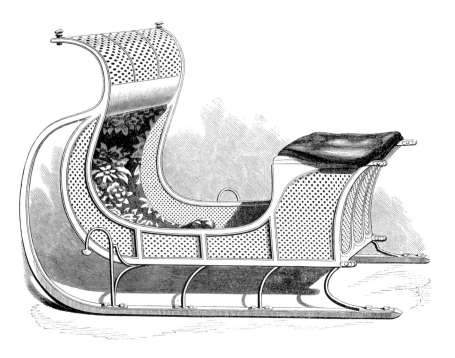

63. *Russian droshki for one person. Catalogue III.*

copies of letters, written in ink, by the mere pressure of the hand', an alarm lock which 'on an attempt being made to pick it, a bell rings, and when the bolt is shot a pistol is fired', a new kind of clock with an alarm called a 'servant's regulator', a clock operated by electric power, a collapsible piano for gentlemen's yachts, a device called the Euxesis for shaving without soap or water, a 'stiletto or defensive umbrella', a pulpit which could be connected to the pews with gutta-percha tubes for the use of the deaf, an expanding hearse by the fashionable undertaker Shillibeer, and a device called the Anhydrohepseterion for stewing potatoes in their own juice. Objects carved laboriously with a penknife seem to have been a topical mania; there was, for example, a model of St Paul's made this way from cardboard, and a carved book-tray 'executed by a ploughman, in the evening, by candlelight, without the aid of any model or design, and solely with a penknife', a set of fruit stones minutely carved by the Duke of Saxe-Cobourg-Gotha, Prince Albert's brother.

France sent in silks and satins from Lyons, linens from Lille, tapestries from the Gobelins and Beauvais, carpets from Aubusson, porcelain from Sèvres, watches from Besançon, enamels from Limoges, *meubles* and *bijouterie*. Germany sent wares from Dresden and Meissen, tobacco pipes, and – in spite of the show's stress on peace between nations – a sinister item from Krupp of Essen labelled 'steel gun, 6-pounder, complete'. From Austria came a display from the imperial printing-office of Vienna of many fine types including Chinese, glass from Bohemia and, among such highly decorated furniture a massive four-poster bed, which the queen purchased, and some pieces made by August Kitschelt in Vienna from wrought-iron tubes. Spain pro-

64. *Large porcelain vase from Russia. Catalogue III.*

duced fans, mantillas and Toledo blades, Switzerland gold watches, muslins and musical boxes, Denmark scientific instruments, glazed paper, patent goloshes, and objects of fine porcelain from the Royal Works of Copenhagen, Sweden and Norway iron ores, silverware, steel razors, a colossal cross cut from a single block of granite, and sixteen packages of stearine candles. Belgium sent lace and Russia wild animal skins, Cossack armour, some giant vases of malachite and porcelain from the Imperial factory, and a mysterious substance exhibited by a peasant described as portable soup. Chile's contribution was a single lump of gold weighing three hundredweight and Brazil proffered a bouquet of flowers made from the wings of native birds and beetles.

An exhibit of popularity that drew continuous crowds, especially the family parties and school groups, were the stuffed animals from Würtemburg, a member of the Zollverein – stoats, weasels, hawks, cats and foxes whimsically arranged in a series of tableaux, a number being based on the old poem of *Reynard the Fox*, beloved of German children. This show was so popular that a children's book based upon it went into several editions during 1851.

An attractive contribution from Canada was a fire-engine faced with copper and having panels adorned with paintings of a great fire in Montreal, of the city's public buildings and of some Canadian landscapes, fire-fighters in Canada at that time being voluntary bodies of young men who took great pride in their engines. The United States accepted more space than it could happily fill, and this closed the end of the foreign wing. Here were mounds of milk-churns, of biscuits, of soap, and of caoutchouc or India rubber, above which the Eagle soared. The first samples of Californian gold were on display; so were Colt's repeating firearms, a sewing machine from C. Morey of Boston, a trotting sulkey so paper-light that a finger could move it, and most impressive of all that McCormick reaper which, set to work on the prairies, would in some years to come knock the bottom out of British farming. There were models of river steamboats, a model of a floating church for seamen, a violin that could be played like a piano with indescribable effects, a giant piano on which four virtuosi could perform simultaneously, some false teeth on an improved principle, twelve Hebrew dictionaries and numerous Daguerreotypes.

66. *Pianofortes by Collards of London. "Industrial Arts".*

India displayed a barbaric splendour with an elaborate throne of carved ivory, the gorgeous coat of a Sikh chieftain embroidered with gold, and covered with pearls, emeralds and rubies, the trappings and a howdah for a rajah's elephant, some magnificent jewellery as well as more prosaic products such as metal ores, tea, coffee, rice and spices. Much was sent in, of course, by the East India Company.

Many examples of misapplied toil and ingenuity were evident in the Great Hive. Among the Philosophical Instruments was 'an apparatus of a peculiar construction, showing the ebb and flow of the tides' sent in by Mr Ryles of Cobridge – 'an apparatus *to illustrate the idea of the earth being a living creature encased in a shell*, as a snail-house or sea-shell, and by the action of the heart (as seen through the glass that is on top of the shell), will contract, causing the tide to rise; let out the air of the shell, and the heart will expand, causing the tide to fall'. The exhibitor added: 'I want a patron that would enable me to show how *the tide causes the rotary motion of the earth*, which only poverty prevents my doing.' A Dr Grey sent in a walking-staff holding medical instruments, medicines and an enema. And there was Count Dunin's 'Man of Steel', a figure constructed of seven thousand pieces, mostly springs and slides, that could be altered from the size of a dwarf to that of a Goliath. Its precise purpose puzzled everyone, yet it received a Council Medal.

Another absurdity was a vase made of lard and mutton fat. Mr Jones of Lombard Street produced 'a silent alarum bedstead to *turn* any one *out of bed* at a given hour', while Mr M'Clintock of York sent in a chain in regular links, the whole of which had been cut out of a solid block of wood.

67. *Willis's grand organ. Catalogue I.*

68. *Austrian gothic bookcase in carved oak presented to the Queen. Catalogue III.*

69. Canadian fire-engine. Tallis III.

It is easy enough to poke fun at many of the exhibits, but thousands of fine, useful things, both labour-saving and labour-creating, were on show, not least in the hardware section with its fire-grates, gas-cookers, cooking-ranges, locks and safes. Applied decoration received a disproportionate amount of attention from the Press compared to the utilities. *The Art Journal*, for example, issued a special catalogue of the highly ornamented Art Manufactures which were lavishly illustrated in masterly wood engravings by the Dalziel brothers (a work recently reproduced in facsimile). Furniture was particularly favoured for these illustrations, most of it embellished on every available square inch, bulging, curvacious and intricate with rocailles. Typical was 'a commode of various woods, the panels ornamented with marqueterie and carvings, and

painted china in the centre; the whole finished with rich gilt mouldings, etc.' In such exhibits the conflict between handicraft and machine production was at its most aesthetically confused and undisciplined, however endearing in these puritan, futilitarian times some of us may find it. The pianos were perhaps the most outrageous in their voluptuous vulgarity. Under the stimulating drug of a reckless romanticism and no longer led by an educated and leisured aristrocracy, taste was out of control. Intricate ingenuity tended to be equated with artistry, and far too many visitors to the Exhibition were enchanted by the apparent sumptuousness that men, machines and money could so rapidly and lavishly supply for those who lived for the pleasure of personal possession.

A court that revealed at least some formal coherence was the Mediaeval, for which A.W.N. Pugin was responsible. Pugin, who had designed the details of Barry's new Houses of Parliament, was an ardent Catholic who regarded the revival of Gothic design as a sacred mission; he was not a brillant architect, but his polemical writings had a profound influence on Victorian architecture. He was a Commissioner for the Exhibition but died insane in 1852. Most of the items in the Mediaeval Court were designed by him and included a great crocketed rood, a high altar of stone, a font, some painted glass, various church ornaments, and a huge square iron stove covered with tiles, coloured, glazed and decorated with heraldry. These things were much admired in spite of the general aversion to the Mother Church of which Pugin was so spirited a child.

The sculpture at the Exhibition was popular too, not least on account of its technical skill applied to narration of the most infantile sort. It was there by the ton, decadent

70. Austria. Dickinson.

71. *German ornamental bird-cage and flower-stand. Catalogue III.*

offspring of Thorvaldsen and Canova, and much of it was either sentimental or surreptitiously carnal. A group of admirers was always to be seen gazing at Hiram Power's *Greek Slave* beneath its red velvet canopy in the centre of the American section. The Catalogue explains the story with care:

'The figure embodies an historical fact . . . and the figure . . . is intended for that of a young and beautiful Greek girl, deprived of her clothing, and exposed for sale to some wealthy eastern barbarian, before whom she is supposed to stand, with an expression of scornful rejection mingled with shame and disgust . . . The chains on her wrists are not historical, but have been added as necessary accessories.' Why the chains should be necessary for the restraint of so cool a character is not revealed. Mr Molony, *alias* Thackeray, decided:

> 'There's statues bright
> Of marble white,
> Of silver and of copper,
> And some of zinc,
> And some I think
> That isn't overproper.'

The largest and most vigorous group of statuary, and the best by any standards, was the vigorous *Amazon attacked by a Tigress* by Kiss, the Prussian sculptor, which was copied in bronzed zinc from the original in bronze erected in 1839 outside the Museum of Berlin.

In her entry for 14 October, the queen wrote:
'After breakfast started for the Exhibition . . . It looked so beautiful and I could not believe that it was the last time I should behold this wonderful creation of my beloved Albert's . . . Walked in fact through the whole building, bidding it regretful adieu. Preparations were already being made for to-morrow's closing ceremony'.

Then, on 15 October:
'This dear day is the 12th anniversary of our engagement! A very wet day. At 10 Albert started for the ceremony of the Closing of the Exhibition, which was not to be in state. I grieved not to be able to be present, and yet I think Albert was right, that I could hardly have been there

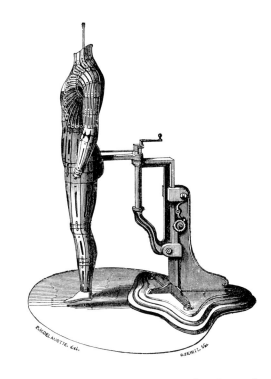

73. *Count Dunin's mechanical figure. Catalogue I.*

as a spectator . . . Albert was back by 2. All had gone off well. Every one seemed pleased. The crowds immense, he thinks from 40 to 50,000 people – closely packed. Albert on the beautiful Indian chair, presented by the Rajah of Travancore, at the head of a table round which sat the Commissioners, all on a platform, read a long answer to Ld Canning, who, as Chairman of the Committee of Jurors, had read a detailed report. A prayer was offered by the Bishop of London, followed by the singing of the Hallelujah,

the whole proceedings having begun with "God Save the Queen" ... To think that this great and bright time is past, like a dream, after all its success and triumph, and that all the labour and anxiety it caused for nearly 2 years should likewise now be only remembered as "a has been" seems incredible and melancholy.'

Finally, on 23 October:

'At 1 had audiences. First knighted ... Mr Paxton, Mr Cubitt and Mr Fox, all of whom seemed quite "emu" and excessively happy.'

The Exhibition had been open for five months and eleven days. On the closing ceremony *The Times* reported:

'As soon as the National Anthem had closed there arose such cheers as Englishmen alone know how to give. These were continued for several minutes, and when the last of them had died away there passed over the entire building, and with an effect truly sublime, a tremendous rolling sound, like that of thunder, caused by thousands of feet stamping their loyalty upon the boarded floors. Under this demonstration every part of the edifice trembled, and, as it swept from west to east, many an eye was raised with anxiety to the girders and pillars, which in long perspective were stretched out before them. And now the time had arrived for the death peal of the Exhibition to be rung out ... At last it came, and a perfect storm of bell peals broke over the building ... It was dark, and half-past 6 o'clock, before the building was completely cleared, and the bells finally ceased tolling.'

A final count showed the total number of visitors to have been 6,201,856, which meant that four million people must have paid one or more visits to the Exhibition – that is well over one and a half times the total population of

74. *The Coventry ribbon. "Industrial Arts".*

75. *The Queen's retiring room at the Crystal Palace. Lloyd.*

London at that time. £356,000 had been taken at the doors, and there was a clear profit of £186,000. How the money was spent, and what happened to the building, will be told in the final chapter.

Every age has its paradoxes but no age was so full of contradictions as the nineteenth century, for it was a century of unprecedented changes and upheaval – economic, social, technical and philosophical. That is evident, not only in the urban environment it formed, but in all its visual design. The schizophrenia of the Victorians is perfectly epitomised in the Great Exhibition. The building itself was a masterpiece; most Victorians thought so and so does posterity. It was a true exemplar of what men like Prince Albert and Henry Cole were so earnestly trying to achieve: the union of Machinery, Science and Taste. The Art Manufactures it contained clearly were not. In their nouveau-riche naïvety, the middle classes confused art with lavishly applied decoration, and this had lost its significance because machines were copying by the yard what could only be done with creative meaning by hand. The Victorians failed to realize, at least consciously, that the machine must produce its own aesthetic. Intellect and instinct were thus at odds.

Neither Ruskin nor Pugin understood this. Yet how puzzling in the confusion of Victorian values are Pugin's admirable principles that would have sufficed as a basic credo for the Functional radicals of the 1930's: 'The great test of architectural beauty is the fitness of the purpose for which it was intended . . . All really beautiful forms in architecture are based on the soundest principles of utility . . . Construction should vary with the material employed . . . Ornament is the enrichment of the essential composition.' Only one man had integrity and he was William Morris. As a youth of seventeen he visited the Exhibition and he was appalled by what he saw. His error, like that of many others, including Pugin, was to retreat into a dream world of the Middle Ages, but at least he did take an uncompromising stand for pure handicrafts as opposed to machine production, and he wished everyone to make and enjoy hand-wrought objects as 'a happiness for the maker and for the user'. The paradox of his situation was that only the wealthy could afford to buy the furniture he made so lovingly by hand; but that was not his fault, it was the fault of the social-economic situation. Morris considered that 'the condition of competition between man and man is bestial' and that it degraded the arts; he did, at least connect:

'A highly gifted and educated man shall . . . squint at a sheet of paper, and . . . the results of that squint shall set a vast number of well-fed, contented operatives . . . turning crank handles for ten hours a day . . . Well, from this system are to come threefold blessings – food and clothing, poorish lodgings and a little leisure to the operatives, enormous riches to the capitalists that rent them, together with moderate riches to the squinter on the paper; and lastly, very decidedly lastly, abundance of cheap art for the operatives or crank-turners to buy.'

Morris could not accept that, for better or worse, the machine had come to stay; he could not see, any more clearly than we can yet, that the end purpose of mechanization must be to emancipate human beings from turning cranks in order that they may return to the pleasures of personal creation through the benefits accruing from ample, machine-granted leisure. Not even the Crystal Palace building itself seems to have impressed Morris. Ruskin loathed it; to him it was simply a 'greenhouse', a 'magnified conservatory', a 'cucumber frame'. So it was in a way, but what a splendid one. It achieved its purpose with complete logic and without benefit of any established architectural traditions. To Ruskin, who became one of the age's arbiters of taste, architecture did not 'admit iron as a constructive material . . . The iron roofs and pillars of our railway stations are not architecture at all.' To the Victorians such structures were Engineering, and there lay a typical Victorian confusion which we have not yet entirely resolved; its apotheosis can still be seen in the extraordinary visual disunity existing between Scott's St Pancras Hotel and the huge train shed to which it is so inconsequentially attached.

To us it seems that the Crystal Palace was one of the greatest architectural monuments ever conceived. It was the one Victorian building, as Sir John Summerson has declared with uncompromising conviction, that was 'a total and absolute success'. Although the Palace impressed them, most Victorians would not have agreed; it just was not Architecture. Not until Walter Gropius produced his Bauhaus at Dessau in 1926 did the old, false notion of the dichotomy between Engineering and Architecture begin to weaken. To the Victorians Architecture meant, above all, eclectic stylism based on academic learning that decorated solid, load-bearing walling in which openings were cut for doors and windows. Their approach to Art Manufactures was the same. Even Paxton accepted the dichotomy, as his 'architectural' designs at Mentmore and Edensor reveal. *The Ecclesiologist*, organ of the Camden Society, commented typically:

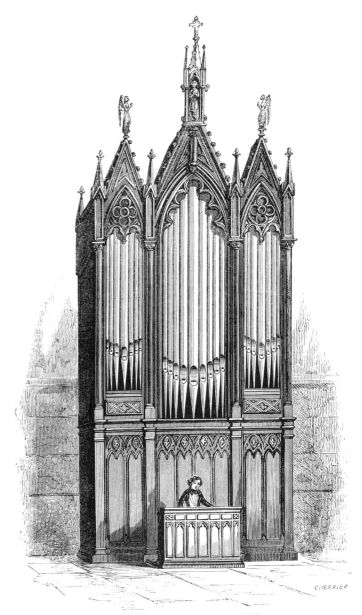

76. *Ducroquet's church organ. Catalogue III.*

77. *Turkey. Dickinson.*

'. . . the conditions under which the Crystal Palace was undertaken could not, we imagine, have been fulfilled in any other way so well as by the execution of Mr Paxton's admirable design. And we freely admit, that we are lost in admiration at the unprecedented internal effects of such a structure . . . a general lightness and fairy-like brilliance never before dreamt of; and above all – to our minds one of the most satisfactory of attributes – an apparent truthfulness and reality of construction beyond all praise. Still, the conviction has grown upon us, that it is not architecture: it is engineering – of the highest merit and excellence – but not architecture. *Form* is wholly wanting: and the idea of stability or solidity is wanting . . . Yet we cannot but feel that the design ought to have been very different in the first instance, had it been intended for permanence. Again: the infinite multiplication of the same component parts – a necessity in such a structure – appears to us to be destructive of its claim to high architectural merit.'

What formed mid-Victorian taste? No doubt the 1832 Reform Act that began to enfranchise the middle classes who created the Industrial Revolution was a major influence. Let Sir Nikolaus Pevsner summarise the situation with his customary clarity:

'The patrons of 1850 were no longer the patrons of 1800. A new class had come to the top and settled down smugly . . . No education and no leisure, these two deficiencies explain nearly all that is aesthetically distressing about 1851. The appreciation of aesthetic values in architecture and design, of proportions, textures, harmonies of colours, requires training and time. The appreciation of the emotional values in painting and sculpture also requires a readiness to listen, to follow a lead and be captured, and this cannot be expected in one whose mind is occupied with machine and counting-house . . . A bulgy curve will be taken in more easily than a delicate one, richly glowing colours than subtle shades, and stories carved in relievo than sheer satisfying proportions. We can say that what appeals to the child, appealed to the big men with the heavy purses in 1851.' (From *High Victorian Design*, 1951).

That the simple, unadorned masterpiece of the Crystal Palace should have been as readily accepted as the many grotesqueries it contained – even if not as 'architecture' – is one of those strange paradoxes in which history abounds.

78.   *The closing ceremony. Dickinson.*

The Dispersion of the Works of all Nations from the Great Exhibition of 1851

79. *The dispersion of the works of all nations from the Great Exhibition 1851. Etching by Cruikshank.*

WHAT ELSE WAS ON?

London in the Exhibition year was in a state of cosmopolitan liveliness it had never known before. Everywhere strange tongues were heard and exotic garments seen, polyglot policemen roamed the streets to assist the foreigners, newspapers printed columns in different languages and new maps and guide-books were published in their tens of thousands. Londoners were on their best and most hospitable behaviour; they tidied up their town and put on a show.

Perennial sights like the Tower of London, the Regent's Park Zoo, and Madame Tussaud's Waxwork Show in Baker Street attracted six times as many visitors as they had the year before. The Imperial Chinese Junk, *Ke-Ying*, that had arrived at Blackwell from the Orient in 1848, was moved by the self-styled Mandarin He-Sing to a new mooring up river at Essex Stairs where his native crew entertained audiences below festoons of lanterns with oriental music, juggling, conjuring, fireworks and vigorous assaults-at-arms, all for a shilling. (At the opening ceremony of the Crystal Palace the droll Mandarin, wearing a robe of embroidered silk and with his long pig-tail swinging below a red cap with peacock's feathers, had created a smiling diversion, swaying from side to side, bowing low to the Royal party and finally taking up a position with august dignity between the Archbishop af Canterbury and the Comptroller of the Household during the progress round the building. He particularly impressed the young Prince

of Wales who requested an immediate introduction to one who was presumed to be an accredited representative. Later investigation proved him to be an enterprising publicity agent for his riverside entertainment.)

One demonstration that stood near the Exhibition was of a serious, philanthropic nature: the model dwellings in the grounds of the Knightsbridge cavalry barracks. Built by command of Prince Albert as President of the Society for Improving the Condition of the Labouring Classes, their purpose was to stimulate the erection of better low-cost housing without pecuniary sacrifice, these particular examples being costed to let at 20p a week each and to provide a return on investment of seven per cent. The small block of four family flats can be seen today in Kennington Park Road on the edge of the park and they

80. *The Chinese junk. "London as it is today".*

are still occupied. The building, designed by Henry Roberts, architect of Fishmongers' Hall and honorary architect to the Society, is in a Tudor gothic style with floors, roof and walls of fireproof hollow brickwork. Although it looks like a cottage, it was so planned that the flats could be repeated if required both upwards and sideways to form a large tenement block. The planning was ingenious and, although the flats were not commodious and lacked bathrooms, they did represent a great improvement on the overcrowded and unhealthy habitations of London's poor at that time and for several generations to come. They are an early example of the welfare tenements of Victorian London erected by such later benevolent bodies as the Improved Dwellings Company and the Peabody Trust – grim blocks of yellow brickwork that only nibbled at the egregious housing problem. Many still survive in London's twilight districts.

Running south of the Crystal Palace, Kensington Gore in 1851 retained a bucolic character with a few large houses set in leafy grounds along the south side. Here was an old turnpike, and a picturesque inn called the Halfway House because it stood where the Albert Hall now rises, midway between the City and the village of Hammersmith. A short distance to its east stood Gore House, a low white, unpretentious Georgian mansion where William Wilberforce had lived at the beginning of the century and in whose library he began his agitation for the abolition of West Indian slavery. In 1821 the gorgeous Countess of Blessington bought the place and there, with Count d'Orsay, she held her literary and political salons to which were invited all the lions of the day, including Louis Napoleon and Charles Dickens. Hounded by creditors,

Elevation.

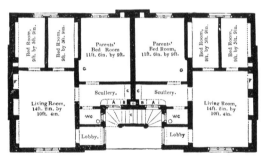

Ground Plan.

81. *Model house for four families built by command of Prince Albert. Catalogue I.*

82. *Duke of Wellington viewing the effigy of Napoleon at Madame Tussauds. Mezzotint by James Scott from a painting by Sir George Hayter; 1852.*

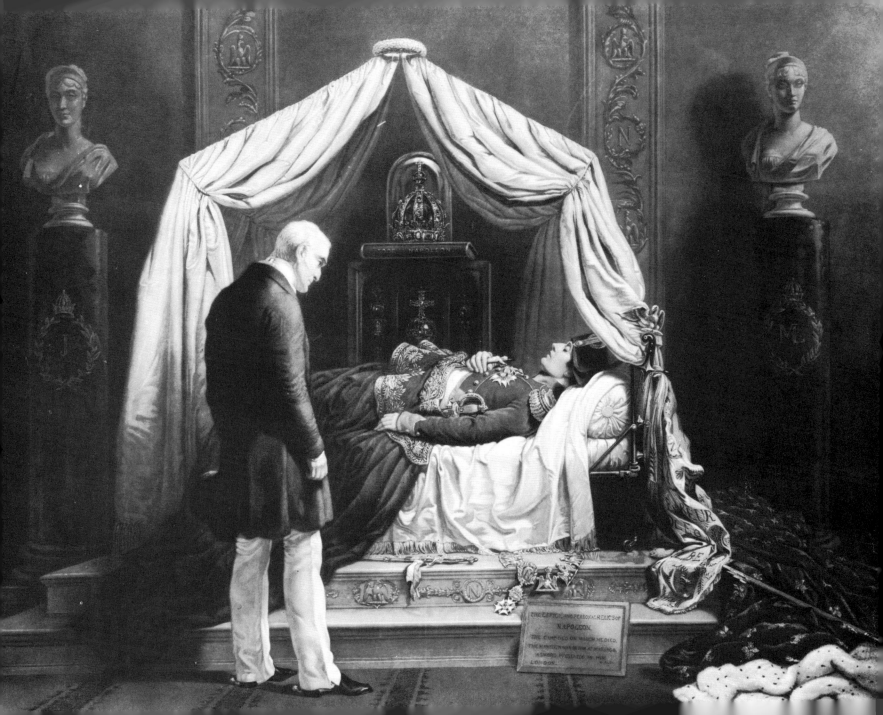

however, the countess was forced to fly to Paris, and then Alexis Soyer, the celebrated French chef of the Reform Club – 'the glory of the edifice' as a contemporary called him – bought the domain with the aim of making his fortune during the Exhibition months with a splendid gastronomical Symposium of All Nations.

Soyer decorated every room in the house with lavish abandon, though with less taste than had its previous occupants. To each room he gave a seductive name: the Blessington Temple of the Muses, the Salle des Noces de Danae all gilt and silver, the sparkling Roscaille of Eternal Snow, the Bower of Ariadne with walls embellished with Italian landscapes, and the Celestial Hall of Golden Lilies in the Chinese manner. The Grand Staircase he decorated with a Macedoine of All Nations, a huge painted medley

portraying the celebrities of the day and conceived by George Augustus Sala who acted for a time as Soyer's assitant. The frondy grazing meadow of eight acres in the grounds Soyer named the Pré d'Orsay, and here he erected the Encampment of All Nations, a dining-saloon containing a table to seat fifteen hundred people covered with a monster cloth of British manufacture over a hundred yards long. In the gardens he also erected fountains and statues, a Grotto of Ondine, a pavilion dripping with coloured stalactites, a Baronial Hall lit by a stained-glass roof, and hung with crimson drapery and oil paintings executed by Madame Soyer.

Soyer charged a guinea per person and three guineas for a family of up to five people, and he often entertained a thousand diners a day. But his outlay had been too heavy and the food, being mass-produced, was not quite good enough for fastidious gourmets. When he closed the place in October, Soyer was £7,000 out of pocket. In 1852 the Exhibition Commission bought the estate as part of the land on which to develop Prince Albert's new cultural area. (Soyer, said Sala, was 'a vain man, but he was good and kind and charitable'. He was also resourceful; he designed the Reform Club kitchens, opened soup kitchens for the poor without solicitation, improved the diet of the troops in the Crimea, in military hospitals and in the emigrant ships. He also wrote several books on gastronomy and died in 1858.)

About a quarter of a mile west of Gore House, facing the end of the Broad Walk in Kensington Gardens where De Vere Gardens now lie, another place of entertainment flourished in the summer of 1851. This was the Royal Hippodrome opened by William Batty, famous proprietor

83. *Ascent of "Erin-go-bragh" balloon at Batty's Royal Hippodrome. I.L.N. July 1851.*

84.   *Grand chariot race at Batty's Hippodrome. I.L.N. May 1851.*

of Astley's Circus in Westminster Bridge Road, who brought over from the Paris Hippodrome a troupe to perform here in a huge oval amphitheatre three hundred and sixty feet long and surrounded by roofed-over seats to accomodate fourteen thousand spectators. During performances two brass bands played alternately in galleries at either end, and the main attractions of the place were for lovers of spectacular horsemanship. Shows included tournaments, Roman chariot races and brilliant historical pageants such as the meeting of Henry VIII with François I on the Field of the Cloth of Gold. Here Mademoiselle Clementine Soulier on her steed Solimon elegantly demonstrated *haute école*, monkeys raced each other on ponies and aeronauts rose in coloured balloons. The Hippodrome survived only for a second season and was eventually used as a riding-school.

A major London show which was initiated in 1851 and lasted for ten years was typically Victorian in its combination of profitable entertainment with altruistic instruction: Mr James Wyld's Monster Globe erected in the centre of Leicester Square. It was the largest model of the earth's surface the world had ever seen.

Wyld was a cartographer and Royal geographer who had inherited – and greatly extended – a map-selling business from his father. He was more than a tradesman and for scientific merit received in his life-time no less than seventeen European orders, including the Legion of Honour; equally, his establishment at Charing Cross was more than a retail shop, for men of standing in the armed and public services regularly resorted there as though it were a kind of club. His youthful but unrealised ambition had been to become a soldier; in 1847, however, he did achieve another ambition in being elected as Liberal Member of Parliament for Bodmin.

Wyld's first idea had been to erect the Great Globe within the Crystal Palace, but its enormous size and a number of technical difficulties rendered this impracticable. He did, however, display his maps at the Exhibition in the section covering Paper, Printing and Bookbinding. He also took a lease on Leicester Square, then an unkempt open space redolent of cats, from the Tulk family who owned the freehold. An architect called Welch was called in to design a suitable building, but his plans were unacceptable and he had in the end to sue Wyld for his fee. Another architect, H.R. Abrahams, was responsible for the building that was erected – an attractive classical one of stuccoed brickwork with four projecting porches in the Doric Order and a lead-covered dome pierced, like the Pantheon in Rome, with an eye at the top. Building went forward day and night for six months, and the place was opened to the public on the 2nd of June, the charge for admission being one shilling (5p).

The globe itself was composed of a thousand plaster-of-Paris casts, each three feet square, supported on ribs of timber, the whole being sixty feet in diameter. The earth was depicted to a horizontal scale of ten miles to the inch, and vertically to one of a mile to the inch; snow was a white incrustation, seas were painted blue, deserts khaki, verdure green and volcanoes had scarlet tips and plumes of cotton wool. Between the lower half of the globe and the external wall of the rotunda ran a passage where maps, panoramas and curiosities were exhibited, its convex wall being painted blue dotted with silver stars in correct astronomical positions. In the centre of the globe (lit by

85. *Wyld's monster globe, Leicester Square. A print by Shepherd.*

gas jets at night), rose a viewing gallery on four stages. The world was, as it were, turned inside out, but since it was on so large a scale and was viewed piecemeal, this anomaly was of little consequence. It worried Mr Punch, however:

'Mr Wyld has made a grand discovery. He has satisfactorily proved that the interior of the globe is not filled with gases, according to Agassiz; or with fire, according to Burnet; neither has he filled it, like Fourier, with water. No, Mr Wyld has now shown us that the interior of the globe is occupied by immense strata of staircases.'

All the same, the Great Globe was a success and remained a metropolitan institution until it was demolished in 1861, when Wyld's lease, which he was unable to renew, ran out.

Leicester Square was the centre of the Panorama entertainment, which by 1851 had become a mania. In London that year were showing not only panoramas, but cycloramas, cosmoramas and dioramas – offspring of romantic landscape painting and legitimate forebears of the cinema, television and the photo-mural. Two distinct forms of this ocular entertainment were developed: the Panorama proper and the more stagey Diorama. The aim of both was to create contrived and spectacular illusions of reality, and it is significant that Daguerre, inventor of photography, was a skilled creator of dioramas before he devoted himself to his photographic discoveries.

The panorama was invented by Robert Barker, an Irish artist working in Edinburgh, who in 1787 obtained an exclusive royal licence for fourteen years. The patent stated that 'after much Study, Labour and Expence he hath Invented an entire new contrivance or Apparatus which he calls La Nature à coup d'œil for the purpose of displaying views of Nature at large by Oil painting . . . or drawing, [and] that he is the first and true Inventor thereof.' The innovation consisted of curving the lines of perspective on a cylindrical surface of the picture so that they would appear straight when seen from a platform built at a certain level at the centre of the cylinder.

In 1793 Barker opened his Panorama on a site lying just to the north-east of Leicester Square, the architect of the building being Robert Mitchell who left a section of his design to show us how it worked. The rotunda, ninety feet in diameter and fifty-seven feet high, was divided into two compartments, one above the other, either to provide a double exhibition or to allow one picture to be painted while the other was on view to the public.

Barker's first show was 'A View of the Grand Fleet regularly moored at Spithead', and thereafter, helped by his son Henry and his assistant John Burford, he produced a long series of panoramas – battles in the Napoleonic wars, Constantinople, Paris, Delhi, and many others. In 1801, when the patent expired, Barker's elder son Thomas built a rival establishment in the Strand, later to become the Strand Theatre. In 1865 the Leicester Square Panorama, now Royal and under the management of Burford's son, was sold to a French priest who built a church on the site for London's French catholic community, doing so on the Panorama's circular plan and using the original wall. This was damaged by bombs in 1940 but the church was rebuilt after the war and the original interior circle of the Panorama Royal can still be seen there today.

The most monumental of panorama buildings was the Colosseum standing where the Royal College of Physicians is now, facing Regent's Park on its south-east corner.

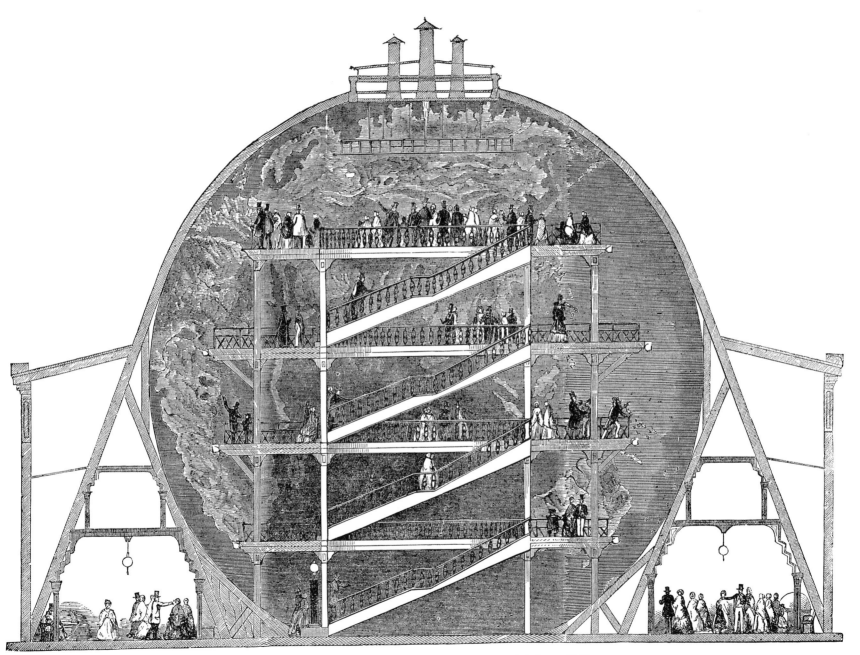

86.   *Sectional view of Wyld's monster globe. I.L.N. June 1851.*

Designed by Decimus Burton and completed in 1826, its original purpose was to display a view of the whole of London as seen from the top of St Paul's Cathedral. It survived until 1875. Like Wyld's Globe, this too was based on the Pantheon, although it was polygonal in plan. A grand Doric portico gave entrance to the rotunda which measured a hundred and thirty feet across, forty feet more than the Leicester Square Panorama, and it was topped by a glazed dome. Sculpture was shown here among other objects, and there was also a large organ. In 1851 the original London view painted by E.T. Parris was still on show during the day, but in the evening it was 'Paris by Night' by Danson and Son. In the grounds stood a crumbling Temple of Theseus and other pagan ruins; also a Gothick aviary, a Swiss cottage, a lake with cataract, and a cavern with stalactites.

Many panoramas were built in London during the nineteenth century such as that in Spring Gardens which gloried in the title: Marshall's Grand Historical Peristrephic Panorama. In 1851 at least a dozen were open. At one you could take a tour from England to Paris; in another you could view 'The Route for Emigrants from Waterloo Bridge Road to the Harbour of Sydney', taking in Lisbon, Gibraltar, Cairo and Calcutta on the way. The original Panorama Royal in Leicester Square was showing the Falls of Niagara and the Lakes of Killarney and Lucerne. Near the Colosseum in Albany Street, the Cyclorama was displaying the Lisbon earthquake of 1755 with moving effects of agitated waves and wildly rolling vessels which, as a guide book explained, reproduced 'the appalling scene in all its attractive horrors'. The Gallery of Illustration in Waterloo Place would take you on the overland route to India all the way from Southampton to Calcutta for the price of a shilling, while for stay-at-homes it also provided scenes of the amusements and employments of English rural life. At that strange Pharoanic fantasy, the Egyptian Hall in Piccadilly, erected in 1812 to the design of P.F. Robinson to house Bullock's Museum, you could follow the ancient Israelites on their way from the Nile to Jerusalem. In Regent Street, the Polyrama was depicting a grand view of Constantinople, while in the Strand, Brees's was showing the Colonies. Most of these spectacles were supported by appropriate organ music.

Just a little way south of the Colosseum, at Numbers 9 and 10 Park Square East, stood London's prototype diorama, a building designed by a Mr Morgan and the elder Pugin and completed in 1823 to house a type of display that was enthralling Parisians. In 1822 Daguerre and Charles Bouton had begun to show their spellbinding tableaux of realistic but dramatised illusions and the following year the London Diorama opened with one of their shows. The diorama was far more effective in its illusions than the less sophisticated panaroma for it was staged in three dimensions and could incorporate movement and cunning changes of lighting, although it never included live human figures. The one at Park Square contained two deep stages set at a slight angle to each other so that while one stage was being prepared the audience by a slight movement of the head could watch the other. In 1851 it was showing Mount Etna under three effects with organ accompaniment: at sunrise, at sunset and in glorious eruption. In 1854 the building was converted to a Baptist Chapel and it survives to this day.

In their *History of Photography*, the Gernsheims quote

87. *Section of the Leicester Square Panorama. Lithograph of 1801.*

Plate 14.

Section of the Rotonda, Leicester Square, in which is exhibited the PANORAMA.

Coupe de la Rotonde, dans laquelle, est l'exhibition du PANORAMA, Leicester Square.

Published May 15, 1801.

Rob.t Mitchell, Architect.

88. The geometric ascent to the galleries in the Colosseum. Lithograph by Ackerman, 1829.

the description of a mystified eye-witness of a typical diorama show: 'A Midnight Mass of St Etienne-du-Mont', one of Daguerre and Bouton's most famous tableaux:

'At first, it is daylight; we see the nave with its chairs; little by little the light wanes and the candles are lighted. At the back of the choir, the church is illuminated and the congregation arriving, take their places in front of the chairs, not suddenly, as if the scenes were shifted, but gradually, quickly enough to astonish one, yet without causing too much surprise. The midnight mass begins. In this reverent stillness the organ peals out from under the distant vaults. Then the daylight slowly returns, the congregation disperses, the candles are extinguished and the church with its chairs appears as at the beginning. This was magic.'

As the Gernsheims explain:

'The 'magic' was achieved by fairly simple though very ingenious means. The picture was painted on both sides of a transparent screen, and the change of effect was produced by controlling the windows and skylights so that sometimes the picture was seen by light shining on the front of the screen, at others by transmitted light from behind, or by a combination of both. In this particular tableau the empty church was painted on the front of the screen in transparent colours, and on the verso in opaque colours the figures of people. In reflected light the empty church alone was visible; the front of the screen was then gradually darkened by closing the skylights, and on opening those at the back the altar lamp and "candles" were lit up and the congregation seemed gradually to fill the church . . . In the following years Daguerre and Bouton went even farther in heightening the cunning illusion of reality by adding actual objects in the foreground. A view of Mont Blanc, for example, contained a genuine chalet, real fir-trees, and live goats, and was accompanied by the sound of cowbells, alp-horns, and folk-songs.'

The summer of 1851 was, of course, a profitable one for the pubs, the theatres and the opera houses. The music hall was still in its infancy, but its father, the great Charles Morton, had already set its precedent at the Canterbury Arms in Westminster Bridge Road, Lambeth, by admitting women as well as men, against convention, to his musical evenings.

Italian opera and the ballet were on at Her Majesty's in the Haymarket and at Covent Garden, and these theatres were patronised by the upper crust – always *de rigueur* in full evening dress. The ordinary theatre at that time was at a low ebb, being of a spectacular, blood-and-thunder character that appealed mainly to the masses. Comedies, poetic plays of a debased tradition and crude melodramas were produced in considerable numbers, and what was lacking in quality was amply made up by quantity. They were the result of the repeal in 1843 of the curious legal monopoly introduced in 1737 that restricted straight drama to the three Patent Houses of Drury Lane, Covent Garden, and, in the summer, the Haymarket. Otherwise, according to the law that was intended to confine legitimate comedy and tragedy, all shows had to contain singing and music. In fact, although the law was obeyed in theory, it was not carried out in practice and many were the subterfuges that enabled the Act to be circumvented. The Patent Houses were all large and so, when the restrictions were removed and all theatres came under the jurisdiction of the Lord Chamberlain, productions, including pantomimes,

89. *Bird's-eye view from the stair-case in the Colosseum. Lithograph by Ackerman, 1829.*

90. *The interior of Her Majesty's Theatre drawn from a model made of cardboard shown at the Great Exhibition. "Art Journal".*

tended to be large scale in their presentations. Companies could number as many as a hundred and the showing of double or triple bills could last from half-past six until midnight; whole battleships and troupes of horses might fill the stage and real waterfalls flow from the flies.

The uneducated audiences of the newly licensed houses did not favour Shakespeare and no good new plays were being written; hence 'The Murder in the Red Barn', 'Raymond and Agnes, or the Bleeding Nun', 'Love in a Maze' and 'I Have Eaten my Friend' were the sort of titles that adorned the bill-boards in their bold Egyptian lettering.

As late as 1882, when the middle-classes were going to the theatre to enjoy new plays about their own lives, the era of the actor-manager was at its height and the Gilbert and Sullivan operas were beginning to swing, Sala as theatre critic of the *Illustrated London News* could describe a sensational drama produced that year at the Globe in a way that might have applied to many of the plays that were being staged in the fifties:

'Take a witches' cauldron and set it over a blue fire: strangle a disreputable junior partner of a money-lender and throw into the pot: hang the other money-lender for murdering his colleague and throw him in likewise: half drown a virtuous young married lady and in with her: beat a small clever child in black stockings very hard to make her tender, and pop her in: add a cup of coffee well poisoned: flavour with a stolen will, a Chubb burglar-proof safe, several forgeries, a good deal of genial humour, an old woman's gingham umbrella, some seaweed from Ramsgate sands, some gravel from a garden on the Thames Embankment, a rasher of bacon from a coffee tavern, a quartern of gin, a Gladstone bag, a small quantity of blood, a pinch of gunpowder, and any amount of vigorous acting, and then you have your bouillabaisse – your "Mankind". Make the gravy very thick and serve hot.'

Finally, the pleasure gardens must be recalled. As a classic eighteenth-century type, Vauxhall on the Surrey side of Vauxhall Bridge was still very much alive in 1851, although it had lost tone and its six acres had become somewhat cluttered with buildings. Vauxhall, in fact, went as far back as the seventeenth century, for Pepys had there seen 'fine people walking, and ladies with masks supping in arbours with mad rogues of the town'. Clarke's *London as it is Today* described the place as it appeared in 1851:

'On the right of the entrance, resplendent with thousands of variegated lamps, tastefully distributed among the foliage of innumerable trees, and festooned in all conceivable varieties of form, is the grand quadrangle, formed of four colonnades, which enclose an open space surrounded with walks and planted with trees, called the Grove, at the centre of which is the lofty orchestra, a magnificent Gothic temple, richly ornamented and glittering all over with many coloured lights, and at the outer extremity are boxes for the accomodation of supper parties; facing the orchestra is a pavilion of the composite order, sixty feet in length, called the Prince's Gallery, in compliment to Frederick, Prince of Wales, who in Vauxhall's palmiest days was wont to sup therein, closing the evening with country dances. The Rotunda is a noble room, sixty feet in diameter, fitted up as a theatre ... The amusements consist of vocal and instrumental concerts ... rope dancing, ballets, and horsemanship in the rotunda; together with dioramic exhibitions and balloon ascents ... closed

91. *Vauxhall Gardens. Contemporary print.*

by a grand display of fireworks, which takes place at eleven o'clock ... Admission, two shillings and sixpence [12½p].'

Admission to Cremorne Gardens higher up river, where the Lots Road Power Station now stands at the west of Cheyne Walk, was only a shilling; it was therefore less select than Vauxhall and was mainly patronised by uninhibited Cockney crowds, students on the spree and provincial visitors who were 'not particular'. The grounds of Cremorne House had become a stadium in 1832 'for the tuition and practice of skilful and manly exercises', but in 1846 it

92. Hansom cab. I.L.N. Nov. 1862.

was opened as a public pleasure garden by Thomas Simpson, a shrewd but kindly man who had been head-waiter at a theatrical tavern opposite Drury Lane Theatre. He built a banqueting hall, a theatre and many secluded bowers. The grounds extended to about twelve acres, to which were added in 1850 those of Ashburnham House to the west. The main entrance was in the King's Road but another was available on a corner by the river for the convenience of visitors who arrived by steamer. According to Sala,

who knew the gardens well, Cremorne, unlike the place Vauxhall had become, was a real *plesaunce* surrounded by fine trees, graced by song birds, flowers and well-tended lawns. The main feature in the grounds was a great orchestra, a Monster Pagoda holding a band of fifty performers and surrounded by a wide platform which could accomodate four thousand dancers.

Diversions were similar to those at Vauxhall (as they were also, indeed, at the Surrey Zoological Gardens that had opened in Walworth back in 1831), but the grounds also became in time more and more congested with side shows. A circus was built, an American bowling alley, a smaller theatre for marionettes, a maze, a shooting gallery and a gipsy tent. Simpson made a success of the place and retired in 1861. Thereafter it gradually fell into decline and acquired a notorious reputation for its parade of prostitutes and the indiscriminate, tipsy pugnacity that became riotous on Bank Holidays and Derby Day. Through the righteous actions of prudes on the prowl it was forced to close down in 1877. The proprietor, John Baum, won a libel case against a man who had openly attacked his establishment in verse and was awarded a farthing damages; he was ill and in debt and did not apply for a renewal of his licence. Soon the green site was smothered by grey speculative houses. Thus this vivacious Victorian resort survived its coeval existence with old Vauxhall by only eighteen years.

93.   *The orchestra at Cremorne Gardens. I.L.N. June 1851.*

AFTERMATH

Two problems faced Prince Albert and the Commissioners when the Exhibition closed: how should the profit be spent, and what should be done with the building? The first was the larger question and Albert took the initiative in solving it. In fact, as early as August 1851, he wrote a memorandum that indicates what was in his mind:

'[In contrast with France and its Central School of Arts and Manufactures] I find that in England the separate pursuits of industry are represented by a variety of public societies struggling for existence unconnected with each other, and either unprovided with suitable locations or exhausting in providing them the funds which should be applied to the promotion of their respective objects. Could not such societies, or most of them, containing as they do all that this country possesses of talent and experience in these branches, be induced to unite in this institution, reserving to each its individuality and self-supporting and self-maintaining character, but bringing them together under a common roof?'

The prince's aim was to promote education under the four main sections of the Exhibition – raw materials, machinery, manufactures and plastic arts – by establishing a centre of trade schools for the stimulation of industry and the improvement in the design of its products. A suitable site for such a centre, lying to the south of Kensington High Road and including Gore House and its grounds, came up for sale. In January 1852 the Commission bought these fifty acres from Baron de Villars for £153,500; additional land was acquired so that the total estate amounted to eighty-seven acres and included twelve acres to the south-east where the Victoria and Albert Museum and the Huxley Building now stand. The main area was

95. *The conservatory in the Royal Horticultural Society's Gardens. I.L.N. July 1861.*

94. *Funeral of the Duke of Wellington in 1852 passing Hyde Park Corner and Apsley House. Ackerman lithograph from a painting by Louis Haghe.*

96. *Sculpture exhibition in the Royal Horticultural Society's conservatory. I.L.N. June 1863.*

bounded by Kensington High Road to the north, Cromwell Road to the south and the new roads of Queen's Gate on the west and Exhibition Road on the east. There today stands a whole group of museums, colleges and other institutions that have made Prince Albert's dream a somewhat confused reality. They include the Royal College of Art, the Imperial College of Science, the Albert Hall, the Royal Geographical Society, the Royal College of Music, the Royal College of Organists, the Royal School of Mines, the Natural History Museum, and the Victoria and Albert and the Science Museums (originally a single entity).

The Government School of Design, a sad failure, was reorganised as a new Department of Practical Art under the Board of Trade to which Henry Cole was appointed Secretary. (Its title was changed in 1853 to Department of Science and Art.) A kind of *Forum Artis cum Academicum* began to form at South Kensington; Albertopolis the scoffers called it; to the prince it was 'Our Sanctuary'.

With Albert's help and support, Cole began to build up a public collection of applied art that eventually became the Victoria and Albert Museum. Its embryo had been the Library and Museum of Manufactures of the Government School of Design established at Somerset House in 1837. At first, part of the collection was displayed in Gore House, but the bulk of it was at Marlborough House, St James's, and it now contained a number of purchases from the Great Exhibition. It grew and, in 1857, a utilitarian structure of iron framework and glass roofing was erected to house it on the site now occupied by the Victoria and Albert Museum. It was officially called the South Kensington Museum but, being a kind of hot house, *The Builder* dubbed it the Brompton Boilers, and the title stuck. The

97. *Design to convert the exhibition building into a tower 1,000 feet high. "The Builder" 1851.*

structure was moved to Bethnal Green and re-opened in 1872 as a branch, while the South Kensington Museum was rebuilt solidly in stages as we see it today. The front, designed by Aston Webb, was not complete until 1909, the year the name was changed. So was formed the finest museum of applied arts in the world, a bureau of design standards that was by no means, even at its start, a hotch-potch of Victoriana, for even during Prince Albert's life many of the acquisitions came from past periods and were rare and beautiful.

The centre of the Commissioners' main site was leased to the Horticultural Society which in 1861 opened a large garden there with terraces, bandstands, basins, fountains and canals, with a fine conservatory or Winter Garden to the north, just south of where the Albert Hall was to be erected and to which it was later attached. Around the garden the Commissioners built arcades and galleries. The Society was compelled to vacate its site in 1882 owing to monetary difficulties. Then it was built over between new cross roads with an accretion of institutions, houses and flats, and London lost another green space.

On the very south border of the site, where the gardens in front of Waterhouse's Natural History Museum of 1881 now lie, London's second International Exhibition was held in 1862 – this time in a great brick structure with the two largest glass domes ever built, dodecagonic in form, rising from it at either end. The sudden death of Prince Albert combined with the Cotton Famine and the effects of the financial crisis of 1857 delayed and blighted the exhibition to some extent, and though it was even larger than the Exhibition of 1851 it was less successful; indeed, it is hardly remembered today. The building was not popular

98. *The suspension bridge at Chelsea.*
Hand-coloured print of 1852.

and was pulled down the following year – and there was no profit. Yet the building had merits, and while it was 'architectural' and lacked the adventure and emblematic significance of the Crystal Palace, it was not without technical interest. Paxton approved of it. Like the Crystal Palace, it was based on a module – at twenty-five feet one foot larger than that of the Palace. The scale was huge – 'something to do with Babylon, some prophesy out of the Apocalypse' as Dostoyevsky described it in his *Winter Thoughts on Summer Impressions.*

Compared with its predecessor, the Exhibition of 1862 showed improvements in machinery but no improvements in taste, in spite of the efforts of Albert and Cole. One important difference was its inclusion of Fine, as well as Applied, Art; it also contained two important contributions that were influential in stimulating the Aesthetic Movement of the seventies and eighties: a large collection of Japanese prints and other objects, and the fresh and charming furniture, embroideries and such works of handicraft presented by Morris, Marshall and Faulkner – the concern William Morris had founded in 1861.

Punch's comment on the 1862 Exhibition was that while the first had been designed by a gardener, this had been designed by a soldier. He was Captain Francis Fowke of the Royal Engineers, a member of an old Leicestershire family born in Belfast. Cole liked to employ the Royal Engineers not only because he was a dedicated civil servant but because in that way he could economically tap government resources. Fowke impressed Cole and he appointed him to superintend the South Kensington buildings. The captain became responsible not only for the Exhibition building but for part of the arcading and other structures around the garden of the Horticultural Society, for the Conservatory to its north, for the Huxley Building at the bottom of Exhibition Road, for a good deal of the permanent new building of the South Kensington Museum and, above all, for the Albert Hall which he did not live to see completed. Fowke was also responsible for the temporary building to house the superb Art Treasures Exhibition held in Manchester in 1857, and he was the winner, under a pseudonym, in a competition for a new Natural History Museum projected for the site of the 1862 Exhibition – a design that was not carried out owing to the captain's demise. Fowke, who favoured a red bricky Renaissance style embellished with terra-cotta ornaments was not the least of Victorian architects; he built economically but not meanly or without flair.

What happened to the progenitor of the cultural district of South Kensington – the Crystal Palace? It had become so popular that many wanted its permanent retention in the Park. All through the exhibition summer schemes for its permanent use were being discussed, sometimes with passion. One notion was to re-erect part of the building in Kew Gardens; another was to re-erect the whole in Battersea Park which would soon be open to the public and be readily approached from the north bank of the Thames by Page's projected Chelsea Suspension Bridge. Both Cole and Paxton wanted to keep it where it was and to convert it into a Winter Park and Garden to provide 'the climate of Southern Italy where multitudes might ride, walk or recline amidst groves of fragrant trees'. Paxton, in fact, produced plans for greatly enlarging the building 'to give a great diversity of views and picturesque effect' where in summer the lower panels would be removed 'so

99. Machinery in motion, 1862 Exhibition. I.L.N. Oct. 1862.

100. The opening of the International Exhibition, 1862. Contemporary print.

as to give the appearance of a continuous park and garden'. A medical man proposed that it should become a Kurhaus 'combining all that in desirable in the spas of Germany with all that is decent in the Roman Thermae'.

The most astonishing proposal, however, came from an architect called Burton, and was published in *The Builder* on 1 May 1852: the conversion of the parts of the structure of the Crystal Palace into a Prospect Tower one thousand feet high 'forming a depository of every branch of art and manufacture our own kingdom produces, as well as a choice collection of exotics from the four quarters of the globe'. As the designer pointed out, the tower would be economical in its use of ground. High up the tower, a clock forty-four feet in diameter would be fixed with figures ten feet long.

But the terms of agreement were clear: the Crystal Palace had to come down. By a considerable majority Parliament agreed. A public company was then formed to acquire the fabric for £70,000 from Fox and Henderson, who had merely rented the structure to the Commission at a low figure, and to rebuild the Palace at Sydenham near the old Beulah Spa on a magnificent hill-top site looking south over an extensive park towards rural Kent and Surrey. The grounds, amounting to two hundred acres, were those of Penge Place, a large country mansion owned by L. Schuster, a director both of the London, Brighton and South Coast Railway and of the Sydenham Company.

Paxton was also a director of the Company and, using the old materials and the same system of construction, he redesigned the Palace on a larger scale that required twice as much glass as the first, contained fifty per cent more cubic space and measured 1,608 feet long. The central apse was larger and higher and all of wrought iron instead of

101. The new Crystal Palace at Sydenham. Contemporary print.

102. *Blondin with his rope. I.L.N. 1861.*

Among the directors, besides Schuster and Paxton, were Francis Fuller, Scott Russell and Matthew Digby Wyatt, all of whom had been associated with the Great Exhibition building. The Chairman of the Company was Samuel Laing, who was also, conveniently, Chairman of the Brighton Railway that ran a branch line to Sydenham expressly to serve the new Crystal Palace. (Eventually the Palace was to be served by two lines from London with Upper and Lower Level Stations.) Fox and Henderson were again the contractors. Paxton was nominated Director of the Winter Garden, Park and Conservatory, Wyatt Director of Works and Owen Jones Director of Decorations.

All concerned were going to improve the minds of the masses with a sugar-coating of entertainment and make a fortune for themselves into the bargain. A thirty per cent annual return on investment was predicted and capital was over-subscribed. But partly because building costs kept rising, partly because Paxton, with an enthusiasm that carried everyone with him, was extravagant beyond restraint (not least in his stupendous system of waterworks in the park), partly because Sydenham lay some way from London's centre and was 'over the water', and partly because the power of the Sabbatarians prevented opening on Sunday – the one day when everyone was free – financial returns never reached expectations. All the same, for many decades the place was immensely popular and for the first thirty years the average number of visitors each year was two million.

A good deal of expense was caused by the slope of the site which necessitated the building of a basement and long, descending terraces with grand Italianate staircases ornamented with balustrades and statues. Heating was

timber framing, and two smaller side apses were added. The new design was undoubtedly impressive but it lacked the serene simplicity of the original. The rebuilt Palace was to be a place for leisure instead of industry – a Palace of the People to provide in the words of the Company's prospectus 'refined recreation, calculated to elevate the intellect, instruct the mind, improve the hearts of, and welcome the millions who have now no other incentives to pleasure but such as the gin-palace, the dancing saloon and the ale-house afford them'.

now necessary as well as ventilation, and this was supplied by a row of twenty-two boilers in the basement to heat water running along nearly fifty miles of iron piping. Down there too, large machines in motion could be exhibited behind an arcade that faced the grounds.

Building began in 1852 and was not completed until 1854, some delays being caused not only by bad weather but by a disastrous accident that took fifteen lives when the scaffolding of the central transept collapsed. Two great water-towers, also serving as chimneys and lookouts, were designed by I.K. Brunel at either end of the huge structure to supply the complex of waterworks with their spouting fountains, cascades, canals, basins, lakes and water temples. These works were intended to rival those of Versailles, and when in full flood required 120,000 gallons a minute to supply some twelve thousand jets.

Paxton regarded the rebuilt Palace as his greatest work and at Sydenham he built himself a home called Rockhill from which he could contemplate his creation. The gardens and park of the Palace he designed with a combination of the baroque symmetry of an Italian prince's garden (no doubt helped by memories of the Grand Tour with his duke) and the informal, picturesque landscaping of an English gentleman's park with its copses, lakes and winding walks. To the planting he contributed all his horticultural skill and knowledge, as though the London public was his aristocratic patron. The public responded with enthusiasm and nervous shareholders protested without conviction.

On an island in one of the two lakes stood a spectacle that drew the crowds from the start – a collection of prehistoric monsters sagaciously fashioned by Mr Waterhouse Hawkins from the available evidence provided by the

103.   *The extinct animals model-room at the Crystal Palace, Sydenham. I.L.N. Dec. 1853.*

104. Opening of the Crystal Palace at Sydenham, 1854. Contemporary print.

naturalists. They can still be seen in the confused and degenerate park that exists today. When the building was nearing completion in 1853, a curious banquet was given by Hawkins in the part of the grounds where his beasts were to stand. As Tallis records:

'In the body of one of the restored antediluvian monsters the repast was spread, twenty-one guests were assembled around the festive board, at the head of which, within the skull of the huge animal, presided Professor Richard Owen, who from that locality delivered an appropriate address on the value of the labours in the wide field of geology and palaeontology of such men as Cuvier, Hunter, and Conybeare. The beast in which he was then speaking (the Iguanadon), had once roamed through the vast forests of Sussex, and had probably perished there through some great convulsion of nature. Many appropriate toasts, and much suitable hilarity beguiled the hours until near midnight.'

In the grounds of the Palace, sports of all kinds could be enjoyed – archery, cricket, football, boating, lawn-tennis and bicycling. There were merry-go-rounds and swings for the children, a monkey house, aviaries, an orangery, a maze and an underground grotto, while near the Rosary at one time was a structure containing yet another of those popular ocular illusions: the Panorama of Tel-el-Kebir by the celebrated Monsieur Philippoteaux. In 1872 a Great Marine Aquarium, four hundred feet long, was added to the diversions. After 1865, when the High Level Station had been built with the entrance arcade of masterly brickwork (still surviving and now under a preservation order), a pneumatic railway was constructed to run through a tunnel for six hundred yards between the Upper and

Lower Level Stations. And in 1865 began a regular London celebration that lasted until the end – the world-famous firework displays that thousands could view to perfection from the broad terraces and staircases on the south of the building.

Whether in the grounds or in the building, something was always going on; in the grounds perhaps a flower show, a balloon ascent or a tight-rope exhibition by Blondin; in the building a mass meeting, a brass-band competition, an opera, circus, or pantomime. 1865 was a particularly lively year and included the Triennial Handel Festival held in the concert hall that seated four thousand people and contained an orchestral platform backed by a mighty organ.

When no great event was taking place or when it was raining, the building – too enormous ever to become overcrowded – offered many permanent entertainments and side shows, and there provender could always be obtained from a bun to a banquet. Cultural instruction was abundant for here were the fabulous antiquarian courts – most of them designed by Sir Matthew Digby Wyatt – that lay on either side of the nave and in the wings. Wyatt was a member of a family prolific in architects, and although not a brilliant designer he was eminently successful: closely connected with the Crystal Palace buildings, Slade Professor in 1869, RIBA Vice-President and so on, who carried out work at Paddington Station and in Scott's Foreign Office and helped to design, with the engineer Rendell, the charming little suspension footbridge in St James's Park now replaced by a modern concrete affair.

The Egyptian Court was the most impressive with its avenue of lions, its sphinxes, its Temple of Carnac and its

105. *The Nubian Court, Crystal Palace, Sydenham. Contemporary print.*

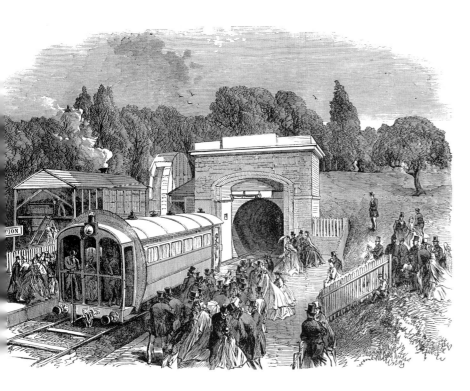

106. *Pneumatic railway for passengers at the Crystal Palace. I.L.N. Sept. 1862.*

pair of colossal Abu-Simbel statues which were so unfortunately to be destroyed in the fire of 1867 that gutted the north transept. Other courts were Assyrian, Roman, Byzantine, Mediaeval, Elizabethan, Renaissance and Industrial. And there was a fine copy of part of the Alhambra, reproductions of the Elgin marbles and of the Raphael frescoes of the Vatican, a model of the Parthenon, the baths of ancient Rome, and, in the Pompeian Court, the house of a Roman citizen in the time of Titus just before the disastrous eruption of Vesuvius.

So the people of Victorian London could find at Sydenham a whole day's relaxation and romantic pleasure – of a sort that previously only the wealthy could enjoy – all for one shilling and sixpence (7½p) a head including entrance fee and return fare.

By the end of the century, the popularity of the Palace began to wane and serious financial difficulties beset the Company. In 1913 the situation was so bad and the fabric in so poor a state that the Nation took over the property. During the First World War it served as a naval depot but, refurbished, it was re-opened to the public in 1920. On 30 November 1936 the Crystal Palace presented its greatest firework display: an apocalyptic blaze that could be seen as far away as Brighton. At nine o'clock came the dramatic opening words of the BBC news bulletin: 'The Crystal Palace is no more'. They shocked the world. Far more than a unique architectural monument had melted in the flames.

The End

107. *A firework night at the Crystal Palace. I.L.N. Oct. 1870.*

108.   *Dinner in the Iguanodon, Crystal Palace, Sydenham. I.L.N. 1854.*

BIBLIOGRAPHY

1. *The Year is 1851* by Patric Howarth (Collins, London, 1851).

2. *1851 and the Crystal Palace* by Christopher Hobhouse (London, 1937 and 1950).

3. *The Great Exhibition, 1851* by Yvonne French (Harvill Press, London, 1950).

4. *The Crystal Palace: 1851 to 1936* by Patrick Beaver (Hugh Evelyn, London, 1970).

5. *The Great Exhibition of 1851: A Commemorative Album* by C.H. Gibbs-Smith (Victoria and Albert Museum, H.M.S.O., 1950 and 1964).

6. *Palace of Industry 1851: A Study of the Great Exhibition and its Fruits* by C.R. Fay (Cambridge University Press, 1951).

7. *The Works of Sir Joseph Paxton* by George F. Chadwick, (Architectural Press, London, 1961).

8. *The Crystal Palace as Structure and Precedent* by P. Morton Shand (*The Architectural Review*, February 1937).

9. *Paxton and Sydenham Park* by G.F. Chadwick (*The Architectural Review*, February, 1961).

10. *Illustrated London News*, 1850 and 1851.

11. *Great Exhibition 1851: Official Description and Illustrated Catalogue.* Three volumes (London, 1851).

12. *The Art Journal Catalogue of the Great Exhibition* (London, 1851).

13. *Dickinson Brothers: Comprehensive Pictures of the Great Exhibition of 1851.* Fifty-five large coloured lithographs from the original paintings done for Prince Albert. Two volumes (London, 1854).

14. *Lloyd's Views of the Great Exhibition.* Coloured lithographs (London, 1852).

15. *Industrial Arts of the Nineteenth Century at the Great Exhibition, 1851* by M. Digby Wyatt. Two volumes containing 158 coloured lithographs (London, 1851-1853).

16. *Tallis's History and Description of the Crystal Palace.* Three volumes illustrated with steel engravings made from contemporary drawings and Daguerreotypes. (London and New York, 1851).

17. *1851: or The Adventures of Mr. and Mrs. Sandboys and Family, who came up to London to Enjoy Themselves and to see the Great Exhibition* by Henry Mayhem etchings by George Cruikshank (David Bogue, London, 1851).

18. *Pictures of Extra Articles and Visitors to the Exhibition* by Richard Doyle (Chapman and Hall, London, 1851).

19. *Prince Albert and Victorian Taste* by Winslow Ames (Chapman and Hall, London, 1967).

20. *The British Metropolis in 1851* (Arthur Hall, Virtue and Co., London, 1851).

21. *London as it is Today: Where to go, what to see, during*

the Great Exhibition (H.G. Clarke, London, 1851).

22. *Mr. Wyld's Monster Globe* by Ralph Hyde (*History of Today*, February, 1970).

23. *London's Lost Theatres of the Nineteenth Century* by Erroll Sherson (John Lane, the Bodley Head, London, 1925).

24. *Cremorne and the Later London Gardens* by Warwick Wroth (Elliot Stock, London, 1907).

25. *The Brick Palace of 1862* by Betty Bradford (*The Architectural Review*, July, 1962).

26. *The International Exhibition of 1862* (Victoria and Albert Museum, H.M.S.O., 1962).

27. *The World's Metropolis or Mighty London Illustrated.* Engravings after Shepherd (Read and Co., London, 1851).

28. *Fifty Years of Public Work* by Sir Henry Cole. Two volumes (London, 1884).

29. *The River Thames from the Palace of Westminster to the Tower.* Lithographs (W. Tegg, London, C. 1858).

30. *1851* by Asa Briggs (Historical Association, 1972).

31. *The History of the Diorama and the Daguerreotype* by L.J.M. Daguerre, edited by Helmut and Alison Gernsheim (Dover Publications; New York, 1968).

ACKNOWLEDGEMENTS

The publishers would like to thank the following for permission to photograph and reproduce books and prints in their possession.

Mr. Ian Hodgkins of Sebastian d'Orsai, booksellers:
    Nos. 21, 22, 29, 30, 35, 69, 72
Victoria and Albert Museum: Nos. 1, 43, 49, 52, 75, 82 and binding
The Guildhall Library: Nos. 6, 7, 11, 12, 14, 27, 31, 32, 36 40, 53, 61, 62, 65, 66, 70, 74, 77, 78
The British Museum: Endpapers
The Parker Gallery: No. 94
Westminster City Library, Buckingham Palace Road:
    Nos. 59, 60, 87
Westminster City Library, Marylebone Road: Nos. 88, 89

All the photographs were taken by John R. Freeman Ltd. The illustrations not listed above are all from the Maré Collection.

SOURCES

The abbreviations in the captions are to the sources listed in the bibliography as follows:

Art Journal: No. 12	Lloyd: No. 14
Catalogue: No. 11	*London as it is Today*: No. 21
Dickinson: No. 13	*River Thames, The*: No. 29
Doyle: No. 18	Tallis: No. 16
I.L.N.: No. 10	*Worlds Metropolis, The*: No. 27
Industrial Arts: No. 15	

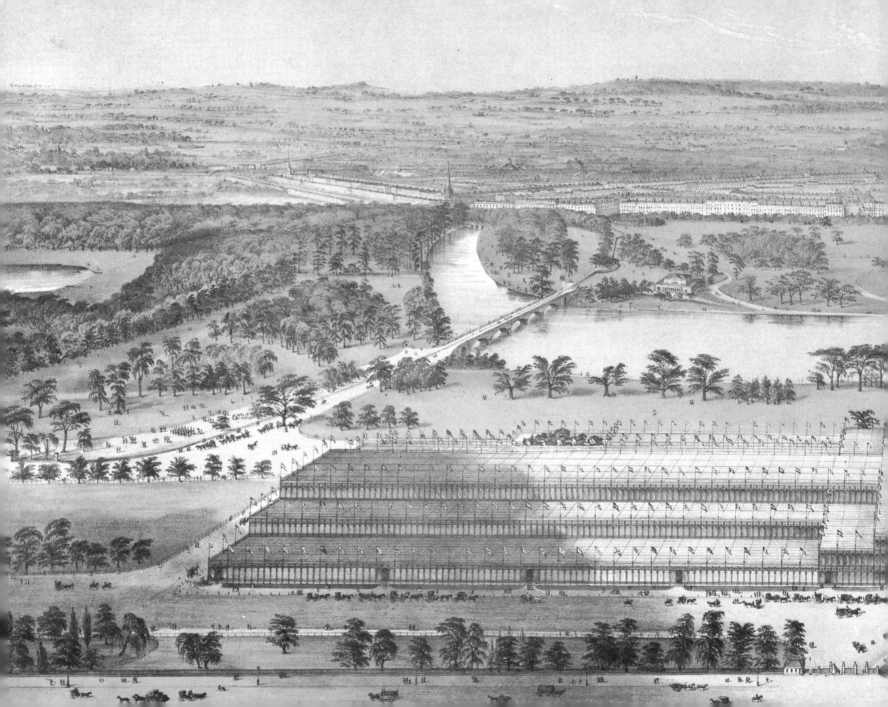